JOWETT, S.

Young disabled people

113,210

D1353742

034590

Young Disabled People:

Their Further Education, Training and Employment

A follow-up of disabled young people from the Further Education Unit at St Loye's College, Exeter

SANDRA JOWETT

NFER-Nelson

Published by The NFER-Nelson Publishing Company Ltd.,
Darville House, 2 Oxford Road East,
Windsor, Berks. SL4 1DF.

First published 1982
© NFER, 1982
ISBN 0-7005-0508-3
Code 8091 02 1

Photoset in Baskerville by Illustrated Arts.
Printed in Great Britain.

Contents

Acknowledgements

I would like to thank all the young people who completed the questionnaires for this study and who welcomed me into their homes for the interviews. They not only made possible the research on which this book is based, but also made it a very pleasant and rewarding experience. The young people's employers also responded most helpfully to their questionnaires.

My thanks are also due to the following individuals: Hazel Benner, Gerald Browne, Steven Dorner, Roger Glanville, Phoebe Lederer, Laurie Moseley, Susan Nath and Alan Walker.

I am grateful to those disablement resettlement officers and specialist careers officers who gave up their valuable time to discuss the research. Daphne Fort and Victor McGuirk of the Spastics Society made useful suggestions.

The staff at St Loye's College were always extremely helpful and their hospitality was very much appreciated. Particular thanks are due to Peter Johnston with whom close liaison was maintained during this project.

Dr Seamus Hegarty as Principal Research Officer provided very many helpful suggestions and constructive criticisms and was involved in the research throughout. Jane Pagett's efficiency and superb secretarial skills were very much valued. Dr Wendy Keys and Christine Moor both gave considerable thought to refining and improving the first draft. Claire Creaser provided the statistical support and efficiently executed the computing.

Special thanks are due to my husband Graham whose constant support, encouragement, understanding, friendship and enthusiasm made the task considerably easier.

Foreword

St Loye's is a training college for the disabled that provides vocational training of various kinds for 150 adults a year. In addition to the vocational provision there is a Further Education Unit which primarily serves a pre-vocational training function for physically handicapped students with potential for employment on the open market. The criterion of likely employability has been the basis of the admissions policy since 1972. Students should be capable of maintaining a job in open employment on successful completion of the further education syllabus and a training course.

As the provision developed, staff felt a need to test the validity of their admissions policy in an objective and systematic way. In its simplest terms, this meant finding out whether clients were getting and keeping jobs. The College cannot be held responsible for the difficulties of the economic situation, and in times of high general unemployment disabled people too must expect problems. On the other hand, the College could not be complacent if very few of its clients were successful in obtaining jobs.

The opportunity to have the placement record examined by an independent source became possible in 1980 with assistance from the European Social Fund. The College had contact with the National Foundation for Educational Research on other matters and asked the Foundation to present a plan of investigation. It is to the credit of St Loye's that the College embarked on a study whose outcome could have had difficult consequences for it – if for instance the number of young people successfully holding down jobs was very small.

The National Foundation for Educational Research was happy to carry out this research not only because of the intrinsic importance of the questions being addressed and the possibility of improving services for disabled young people but also because of the opportunity it afforded to build on existing work at the Foundation in this sector. A number of studies into FE provision for those with special needs had been carried out while others were still in train. The present project made it possible to add to these studies by looking in detail at the situations of a specific group of young people and examine the impact of specialist provision on their lives. An added bonus was the opportunity afforded of examining these issues from the perspective of the young people receiving services. Moreover, no systematic follow-up study of this group had been carried out, and this study would help in filling a major gap in our understanding of services for disabled young people.

The study itself lasted for a year and was conducted in 1980/81. The twin aims were (i) to examine the vocational and social progress of a specific group of disabled young people who had left the training college and (ii) to relate this information to their experiences within the Further Education Unit at the training college. Questionnaire data and a wide range of interview material were drawn upon to give an account of the young people's experiences in getting and keeping work, the significance of work in their lives, their social and emotional development, their views of the training they had received and many other topics.

The findings on the employment record may be of most immediate interest – two thirds had obtained open employment but not all had kept their jobs – but numerous issues bearing on employment as well as more general matters are discussed here. The former include the relationship between training course taken and subsequent employment history, the Youth Opportunities Programme, job satisfaction and wages earned. Getting a job raises particular problems for these young people and the balance between individual or parental initiative and the contribution of the professional placing services is considered. More general matters discussed include the social and emotional development of the young people in question and their growth as independent adults. The young people made some pertinent observations about their training and its relationship to their present situation. While these comments were specific to St Loye's they contain implications for the organization of further education provision for disabled young people that have more general relevance. It is particularly valuable to have these discussed in the context of the actual experience in early adult life of a sizeable group of disabled young people.

Seamus Hegarty

Young Disabled People: Their Further Education, Training and Employment is the Report of the Project 'The Placement of Disabled Young People from a Further Education Unit', undertaken at the National Foundation for Educational Research in England and Wales.

This Project received financial assistance from the European Social Fund; however, the views expressed by the promoter are not necessarily those of the Commission of the European Communities.

CHAPTER ONE

Introduction

St Loye's College for Training the Disabled for Commerce and Industry was established in 1937 and is a voluntary organization registered as a charity. It is one of four residential specialist training colleges financed by Government grants for its running costs and depending on charitable income for all capital expenditure such as new or improved buildings, furnishings and equipment. It is situated on the outskirts of Exeter in Devon and enjoys a very pleasant campus with extensive grounds. The Further Education Unit is a purpose-built, quite separate part of the college with its own residential block. Also on site are the College's sheltered workshops and the St Loye's School of Occupational Therapy.

The College's Annual Report (1979–80) details its aims and organization:

> it began with the object of proving that severely disabled people could be trained to compete on equal terms with the able-bodied;
>
> it has successfully trained over 10,000 men and women for open employment in commerce and industry;
>
> it offers residential training for 150 men and women on a wide variety of skill courses and 60 boarding places for handicapped school-leavers requiring further education, assessment and pre-training;
>
> trainees and students suffer from all types of physical disability, other than total blindness, and come from all parts of England, Scotland and Wales.

St Loye's College receives financial and technical assistance from the Manpower Services Commission (Training Services Division) and offers a comprehensive range of training courses which are intended to lead to full open employment in commerce and industry. There are no formal entry requirements for the various courses and the aim is to develop potential rather than to have entry standards which sometimes have the effect of excluding those with under-developed talent. A booklet prepared by the Manpower Services Commission giving details of the courses emphasizes that their design is not rigid, that extensions of time can be arranged if necessary and that transfer to another course is possible. The notes available for each course indicate restrictions for entry that relate either to the physical disability of applicants, for example hearing impaired people are not suitable for the audio-typing course, or to the physical limitations a person may meet in their working environment – people confined to wheelchairs may find difficulty in obtaining work using Data Preparation skills due to the size and location of the machines used. The examinations that may be taken by those on each course are also listed. Brief details of each course and its duration, taken from the MSC's booklet, are given below.

Courses in commercial skills

Basic Office Skills (6 weeks): a course in general office routine and instruction in the use of the more common office machines. All trainees undergoing clerical training are required to take this introductory course.

Audio-typing (20 weeks): provides training in typewriting and the use of audio equipment – includes tabulation, display and working from amended manuscripts.

Book-keeping and Accounts (26 weeks): prepares for the duties of accounts clerk employed in commerce.

Copy-typing (16 weeks): designed to produce clerical workers who are able to perform most routine tasks required in offices.

Hotel reception duties (26 weeks): a composite course in general office duties, typewriting, telephone switchboard operating, elementary book-keeping and the use of accounting machinery, some knowledge of catering control and work experience in a hotel reception office.

Data Preparation (20 weeks): provides training in the operation of modern conventional computer data input material.

Shorthand and typing (39 weeks): Pitman's '2000' shorthand and typewriting are taught. Instruction provides for normal commercial correspondence, tabulation, display and working from amended manuscripts.

Telephony/typing (16 weeks): trains in the operation of all current types of telephone switchboard. Typewriting is excluded in cases where it is physically impossible for a person to operate a typewriter and then the course is of 12 weeks' duration.

Courses in technical skills

Basic Workshop Practice (3 weeks): this is the first three weeks training in the following trade courses (excluding the last three). Trainees are familiarized with the tools and materials of their prospective trades. This three weeks is included in the number of weeks indicated for each course.

Electronics wiring (20 weeks): a course in industrial electronic wiring technique and practice designed to meet the employment requirements of most manufacturers in the electronics industry.

Engineering inspection (20 weeks): prepares for employment in the engineering industry as Inspectors of precision-made components and assemblies, checking for correctness to drawings and other specifications, interpreting drawings, and using gauges and measuring instruments.

Joinery (26 weeks): the use of tools, production of good class joinery and satisfactory work output are the training aims of this course.

Light electro-mechanical fitting (36 weeks): provides a basic skill in the fitting and assembly of small mechanical and electro-mechanical devices and in the manufacture of replacement components using light machine tools associated with instrument making.

Light precision engineering (36 weeks): provides training in bench fitting and machining leading to employment in light engineering where close tolerances are essential.

Radio, television and electronics servicing (52 weeks): aims to produce improver grade technicians capable of maintenance, fault diagnosis, and repair of radio receivers, televisions, tape recorders and record players.

Watch and Clock repair (52 weeks): a course in the maintenance and repair of timepieces of all kinds, which includes the manufacture of certain replacement components using hand tools and the watchmakers' lathe.

Cookery (Industrial) (26 weeks): a course in all aspects of quality food preparation, cooking and serving.

Horticulture (52 weeks): a comprehensive and practical course in all the usual aspects of vegetable production, care of lawns, borders and shrubberies, glasshouse management, propagation methods, use of fertilizers and insecticides and the operation of grasscutting and light cultivating mechanical equipment.

Storekeeping (14 weeks): this provides the practical and theoretical instruction in the maintenance of store records, use of standard stores documents and day-to-day stores operation.

The Further Education Unit

Services to promote the employment opportunities of disabled people have been established in response to the needs of those who become disabled during their working lives, notably during service in the Armed Forces. The development of St Loye's College is in keeping with this trend. A large majority of disabled people have become disabled as adults. The emphasis on services available to disabled people is indicated in the title disablement resettlement officer – the Manpower Services Commission's officer whose role was originally envisaged as resettling in industry people who had been the victims of disabling accidents, injury or disease in adult life.

Young people who have been disabled from birth or early childhood are in a rather different position in that they may need specialized education and training to enable them to make a successful transition from school to work and yet would be inappropriately placed in one of the training courses at a college such as St Loye's. It was in response to the needs of young disabled people that the Further Education Unit at St Loye's was developed. In the early 1950s young people applying to the College were thought to be in need of a pre-vocational course of a rather different nature from that provided for the adult trainees and the Unit grew from a situation where four boys were taught by one member of staff in a part of the main college to the present arrangement whereby up to 60 young men and women are taught in a purpose-built Unit by a team of staff. Students in the Unit are financed by discretionary grants from their Local Education Authority. After a three-term foundation course the majority of students in the Further Education Unit spend a fourth term on a specific pre-training course before moving over to a course in the main part of the College. In fact 70 per cent of the young people in this study made this move. For those not considered suitable for a training course there has been available (since 1978) a Work Preparation course that occupies their fourth term. This course which includes a period of work experience aims to prepare young people more directly for entry to open employment. The majority of young people attend the Further Education Unit for four terms though this period may be shortened or extended to five terms where it is considered appropriate.

As with the adult training side of the College, there are no formal entry requirements for the Further Education Unit. Many students have however obtained a small number of CSE (Certificate of Secondary Education) passes. Students are admitted to the Unit on the basis of a 24-hour assessment held at the College. These assessments are held every Thursday during term time and up to three applicants may be assessed at any one time. The applicants generally arrive at the College on the evening before their assessment day and spend the night in the Unit's residence. They have an opportunity to meet those currently attending the Unit and the residential staff are able to gain an impression of them.

The following day applicants are assessed in terms of their technical and commercial skills potential and their present attainment in English and maths. They are interviewed by members of staff, who later discuss the application with the parents or escort. This assessment period is designed to identify young people who would be able to benefit from a period in the Further Education Unit and to then transfer to a course in the College that would lead to open employment. The applicants' abilities – both physical and educational – are assessed and consideration is given to personal factors such as their attitude and apparent motivation. Sixty per cent of the young people assessed at the College are offered a place and the staff are aware of the difficult decisions they have to make. Some issues relating to the assessment of disabled school leavers are discussed in Chapter Seven.

During their foundation year in the Unit the young people's day is divided into sessions for Maths, English, General Studies and Technical and Commercial skills with 40 per cent of their time being allocated to these last two. All the young people start in this way and it is anticipated that some time after the first half of their first term their training 'bias', i.e. Commercial or Technical skills, will be clear. It is felt that the potential of many young people may be under-developed and that they need to be considered for all the courses available to them. Identification of the 'bias' enables the curriculum to be related more narrowly to each young person's eventual training trade.

The General Studies course offers young people an opportunity to study topics that may be unfamiliar to them such as computer studies, money management, technical drawing and photography, and enables them to develop more generally applicable skills of independent work and study. Students have considerable freedom as to which topics they choose. All young people in their fourth term now have a weekly session concerned with issues related to work. The comments of the young people on the curriculum are detailed in Chapter Six and the importance they attached to such work-related skills is discussed.

This research

In order to collect the information required it was decided to follow up all those people who had entered the Further Education Unit at St Loye's between January 1974 and December 1978. There were 189 young people available to provide information for this study. A small number of entrants were excluded either because they had died, they were still involved in training at St Loye's, they had only stayed in the

College for a very short time, or, in the case of one young man, they were serving a prison sentence.

The 189 people were contacted by a letter which explained briefly the aims of the research and invited them to participate. A tear-off slip at the bottom of the letter was provided and the young people were asked to return this giving their correct address. Such initial contact would, it was hoped, provide some idea of the number of people who were untraceable (bearing in mind that some addresses were six years old) and would verify or correct the remaining addresses. Where this first letter was 'returned to sender' attempts were made via the Social Services and the Employment Services to locate the young person. Such attempts were successful in a few instances, reducing the number of those who were not able to be contacted for this study to twelve.

The Questionnaire

The remaining 177 young people were each sent a questionnaire consisting of 32 questions. A small pilot study involving people who had entered the Further Education Unit in 1973 had indicated that the questions were unambiguous and the answering scheme usable. The first 20 questions sought information about work undertaken, use of placement services and periods of unemployment. Respondents were invited to comment retrospectively on the Further Education Unit in questions 21 to 29. The remaining questions were concerned with the respondent's health, their perceived difficulty in certain social situations and whether or not they were registered with the Department of Employment as a disabled person. (The questionnaire appears in Appendix A.)

There was a most gratifying response rate to these questionnaires. Well over half were returned completed from the initial approach and the final response rate was achieved using two follow-up letters sent at two-weekly intervals, the second one enclosed with a further copy of the questionnaire. The response rate was

153 completed questionnaires;

4 questionnaires returned with a covering note stating that it had been decided not to complete them;

9 people whom it was known had had a questionnaire sent to their correct address who had not returned it;

11 people who had not returned a questionnaire and whose address had never been verified.

The response rate calculated most rigorously, i.e. the percentage of completed questionnaires in terms of all potentially possible returns is 86 per cent. It is certainly possible that those people in the last group did not receive a questionnaire and the response rate calculated on this assumption is 92 per cent. What is clear, is that only 9 people were known to have received a questionnaire and to have not responded to and returned it. This positive and encouraging approach to the research was perhaps well-illustrated by one young man who completed and returned both the initial questionnaire and the one enclosed with the second follow-up letter and the young woman who when interviewed expressed surprise that there was such a thing as a return rate exclaiming 'Do you mean to say some people didn't fill one in?'

The quality and quantity of information to be gleaned from the completed questionnaires varied greatly. All 153 were usable and the vast majority of respondents had accurately completed all the questions requiring them to circle the correct answer. The differences in response were most evident in the questions that required both considerable thought and fluency on paper. One question for example asked respondents to rate their time in the Further Education Unit on a 4-point scale that ranged from 'Happy most of the time' to 'Unhappy most of the time'. Only one respondent did not complete this part of the question. However the next part which asked 'Why was that?' prompted a variety of responses ranging from the 16 per cent of respondents who wrote nothing to the 3 per cent who wrote a paragraph detailing four contributory factors. A few questionnaires were very scantily completed, and others were filled in with a competence that indicated that considerable thought, time and effort had been expended. Lucy, a young woman with spina bifida who was confined to a wheelchair and working successfully as a telephonist/receptionist, filled all the available space on the questionnaire with her precise, neatly rounded words and then carefully stapled on slips of paper to indicate that what was written on these slips while relevant to the adjacent question was slightly tangential!

The Interviews

Collecting information by questionnaire has obvious limitations.

Collecting information by interviews should provide an opportunity to 'flesh out the bones' of the basic, mainly factual, information obtained from the questionnaires. To this end, 34 of the young people who had already completed questionnaires were interviewed. The willingness of the young people to participate in this study was again confirmed by the fact that only two of those approached for interview withheld their consent.

The people approached for interview were selected to reflect the distributions of sex, disability and vocational training received (if any) of the population. There were constraints of time and distance that determined who and how many, but within these constraints a balance was maintained. The interviews were conducted at the interviewee's home (with one exception where it was undertaken at the interviewee's work-place), and were held in nine counties of England and Wales. The majority of interviewees lived with their parents, though six people were seen in rented accommodation, one in lodgings, and one in owner-occupied housing. There was one joint interview where a husband and wife who had met while at St Loye's were visited.

Those interviewees who were currently in employment or who had worked since leaving St Loye's were asked in more detail about their work and those who were unemployed were asked about how they spent their time and their job-hunting. All interviewees were asked further questions about St Loye's and new issues were raised such as social contacts, attitudes to disability, independence and possible worries or fears.

It would be fair to say that all those young people interviewed gave freely and willingly of their time. Most seemed to enjoy this opportunity to talk to someone about their experiences and perhaps being asked for their opinions was something of a novelty. The warmth and obvious enthusiasm with which they approached the interview seemed in many cases to contrast sharply with the contents of the interview which described social isolation and the boredom and frustration of unemployment. All the quotations used in the text are verbatim.

Most of the interviews lasted for between two and two and a half hours, the shortest being for one and a half hours and the longest for three and a half hours. All the correspondence for this study had been addressed to the young person concerned which seemed reasonable since a fundamental aim was to find out how the recipients of a service felt about it. Given an age range of interviewees of 18–23 years this

seemed practicable. At the time of interview any parents present were informed that questions had been devised for their son or daughter and were invited to make any comments they had at the end. Most parents felt able to do this, but a few seemed to have considerable difficulty in disengaging from the interview and such difficulty could well extend to other areas of family life and have implications in terms of the 'child' being treated as a young adult. The issue of independence – of which this is one facet – is raised in Chapter Five.

The Employers

The questionnaire that went out to the young people had a space for those currently in employment to write their employer's name and address and to indicate whether or not their employer could be approached and asked to complete a short questionnaire. Most people in employment gave their consent with the result that 56 employers were sent a questionnaire and invited to participate in this study. The questionnaire was only sent to the employers of young people in open employment or on Youth Opportunities Programmes as the information sought was not relevant to those in sheltered work or day centres. Again there was a gratifying response with 84 per cent of questionnaires being returned completed, the majority of these from the initial contact. Indeed 12 questionnaires arrived back by return of post. Many employers provided information in addition to the requirements of the questionnaire. One included reports completed by three colleagues of the young person in question and three made personal contact by telephone to discuss the issues more fully.

Employers were asked about the placement and work performance of the young person in particular; they were also asked more generally about their experience of employing disabled people. The questionnaire used appears in Appendix B, and the answers they gave are discussed fully in Chapter Two. The very positive comments made by employers may come as a surprise to some people who have a limited experience of disabled people at work. Stereotypes simplify our dealings with other people and, once established, tend to persist.

The next five chapters detail the findings of this research. Chapter Two describes the employment histories of young people, the relationship between training courses and employment and the comments of their employers. The other four chapters deal with the situation of unemployed young people, the meaning of work, the young people's experience of job placement services, their personal development and their views and comments about the Further Education Unit. A summary of the main points is provided at the end of each chapter and all the summaries appear in Appendix C. The final chapter discusses wider issues that relate to the needs of disabled young people.

CHAPTER TWO

Young People and their Placements

Detailed information was available about the experiences of 153 people in the time since they left St Loye's. Their placements are discussed in this chapter and there are separate sections on open employment, sheltered employment, Youth Opportunities Programmes, day centres and adult training centres and voluntary work. Information is provided about the work experience of young people in terms of the training course taken. The responses of the young people's current employers provide another important perspective. It is anticipated that the figures and the trends they indicate will be of interest, but they must be interpreted with care. The findings present an accurate picture of the placements of all the young people who entered the Further Education Unit over a five-year period, but the numbers involved are relatively small. A further caution arises from the necessity to view the figures in the context of continuing high levels of unemployment. Recent unemployment figures available from the Manpower Services Commission (March 1981) indicate a rate of 10.1 per cent for the general working population and 15.3 per cent for disabled people. In a recent report by the Further Education Curriculum Review and Development Unit (1980) it was suggested (p. 81) that an emphasis on the individual may be inappropriate in view of continuing unemployment and comment was made on the possibility that one might achieve employability but still be unemployed because of the state of the economy.

Characteristics of the young people

Apart from the obvious differences in personality and outlook the 153

respondents to the postal questionnaire differed in certain quantifiable ways that are detailed below. The young people in this study had
for example travelled a range of distances from their homes to join the
college. A few had come from Exeter and its immediate surroundings;
a few had homes in the North of England or indeed North of the
Border. Forty-six Local Education Authorities had financed the
further education provided and most had involvement with just one
or two young people, although there were three LEAs that had spon-
sored 72 school leavers between them.

The young people varied tremendously in both the nature and
extent of their disability and Table 2.1 gives some details. Figures are
given both for respondents and for the total population of this study,
i.e. all the young people who entered the Further Education Unit
between 1974 and 1978.

**Table 2.1: People with different disabilities amongst
(a) the respondents (n=153) and (b) the population (n=189)**

Disability	(a) $n=153$		(b) $n=189$	
	%	Actual number	%	Actual number
Upper-limb disability	3.3	5	4.2	8
Lower-limb disability	2.6	4	2.6	5
Paraplegia	2.6	4	2.1	4
Other spinal disabilities	3.3	5	3.2	6
Arthritis	2.0	3	2.1	4
Cardiac	5.9	9	4.8	9
Epilepsy	10.5	16	10.6	20
Hemiplegia	13.1	20	11.6	22
Hearing impairment and communication disorders	7.8	12	6.8	13
Cerebral Palsy	5.2	8	4.8	9
Muscular dystrophy	2.0	3	1.6	3
Spina bifida†	10.5	16	10.1	19
Visual handicap	6.5	10	6.3	12
Alimentary	3.9	6	3.2	6
Diplegia	6.5	10	6.9	13
Arthrogryposis multiplex congenita	2.6	4	2.6	5
Other‡	11.8	18	16.4	31

† Included in this group were three young people with hydrocephalus and
three with arrested hydrocephalus.
‡ Included in this category were disabilities such as haemophilia, spinal
muscular atrophy, minimal brain damage and Friedreich's ataxia.

About 20 per cent of the young people had a secondary disability. The main secondary disability was epilepsy which accounted for a quarter of all such disabilities. The respondents differed from the total population in terms of disabilities in that there were rather more people in the 'other' category in the population though this difference was not statistically significant. The only other difference of note between the respondents and the population was that proportionately more people in the latter group had only had one or two terms in the Further Education Unit.

Table 2.1 shows the medical classification of each person's disability, but does not indicate the degree of functional impairment. A person may, for example, be classified as having cerebral palsy and may have a functional limitation in only one limb. Another person similarly classified may be confined to a wheelchair. In order to clarify the extent of the disabilities of the young people taking part in this study two of the professionals concerned with their care and education at St Loye's were asked to score each person in terms of his or her limitations as regards verbal communication and mobility. They also scored the visibility of each person's handicap. Such a method undoubtedly has limitations especially as it deals with the raters' retrospective perceptions, but nevertheless it was felt that some measure of functional disability was necessary. Each of these three characteristics was scored on a scale from 1 to 5 where 1 indicated no deviation from the norm and 5 severe deviation. The scores given by the two raters were averaged and the respondents were then split into three groups for visibility of handicap and impairment of mobility and two groups for impairment of communication.

Details of the groupings are given in Table 2.2.

The groupings for visibility of handicap and impairment of mobility were made so that a person in group A would have scored 1 from each rater or (for three people) 1 from one rater and 1/2 from the other. Someone with epilepsy or a heart condition, for example, could score A in each as their disability would not affect their mobility or their appearance. Those people in group B had scored between 1.5 and 2.5, though the most common score in each case was 2. Someone with an unusual gait could score 2 in either of these categories. Those people in group C scored above 2.5 (in all but four cases at least 3). Such a score, for impairment of mobility, would indicate someone who regularly used calipers and crutches or a wheelchair. As regards visibility of handicap, someone in this group could, for example, suffer from a severe skeletal deformity. The impairment of communication scores were grouped so that those people in group A scored 1 or (in the case of 13 people) 1 from one rater and 2 from the other. Those in group B include people with speech defects, hearing disorders and aphasia.

Table 2.2: Functional aspects of disability (n=153)

Visibility of Handicap		*Impairment of Mobility*		*Impairment of Communication*	
Grouping	% in group	Grouping	% in group	Grouping	% in group
A 'invisible' handicap	27	A 'normal' locomotion	39	A unimpaired speech	86
B mild deviation from the norm	55	B limited mobility	45	B communi- cation disorder	14
C severe deviation from the norm	18	C severe restriction on mobility	16		

Only 16 per cent of the young people were classified as having severe restrictions on their mobility and only half of these people were confined to a wheelchair. A recent study (Weir, 1981) commented on the tendency to think of wheelchairs when disability was mentioned. This would clearly mis-represent the young people in this study. It is estimated that in the general population only something of the order of 2 per cent of those people classified as disabled are confined to wheelchairs. It is also worth noting that the use of phrases such as 'wheelchair cases' for people who are confined to wheelchairs and 'E.P.s' for people who suffer from epilepsy may do little either for the self or public image of disabled people. Similarly the much-used phrase 'The Disabled' mis-represents the vast range of people who in one way or another are handicapped in that it implies a commonality of life experience, personality, intellect and needs. Talking about people as a group may sometimes be convenient, indeed essential, but it does stress similarities at the expense of individual differences.

At the time that this information was collected the young people's ages ranged from 18 to almost 25 years. Thirty-seven per cent of the respondents were young women and 63 per cent were young men.

This distribution of the sexes may reflect attitudes that further education and training is somehow of more importance for male school-
leavers. As regards previous schooling, 53 per cent of the respondents
had attended ordinary school, 28 per cent attended a special residential school and 18 per cent a special day school. Two young people had
had home tuition.

Young people were selected for interview to provide as representative a sample as possible. Twenty-two young men and 12 young
women were interviewed and their ages ranged from 18 to 23. Four
young people had trained in telephony/typing, six in book-keeping
and accounts, two in data preparation and one as a typist. Three
young men had trained in electronic wiring, five in store-keeping, two
in horticulture and one in joinery. Of the ten interviewees who had not
taken a training course, three had done a Work Preparation term in
the Further Education Unit. Fifteen of the interviewees were in
open employment, one was in sheltered work, one on a Youth
Opportunities Programme and 17 were unemployed.

Six young people in the sample had spina bifida, five had epilepsy,
three had cerebral palsy and three had a hearing impairment or communication disorder. One young man was visually handicapped,
another was a thalidomide victim and another had suffered extensive
burns. Other people interviewed suffered from muscular dystrophy,
Friedreich's ataxia, arthrogryposis multiplex congenita, muscular
atrophy and dwarfism. A medical atlas edited by Bleck and Nagel
(1975) is a useful reference text.

A summary of placements

The present situation: At the time that this information was collected
rather less than half of the respondents (44 per cent) were working in
open employment, 43 per cent were not working at all and the remaining 13 per cent were involved either in Youth Opportunities Programmes, sheltered work, day centres and adult training centres or
voluntary work. The figures are detailed in Table 2.3.

A clear distinction has been made in this report between the various
types of employment. Open employment is employment in ordinary
organizations and firms where the disabled employee works alongside
able-bodied employees, whereas sheltered employment is intended
for disabled people who are not able to work in open employment but

are nevertheless capable of productive work. Youth Opportunities Programmes (YOPs) which are government-sponsored schemes for unemployed young people were classified separately. Day centres, adult training centres and voluntary work were also held to be quite separate categories of occupation. Those people who are classified as unemployed are not taking part in any form of structured activity outside their home.

Table 2.3: Present occupation

Occupation	Actual number involved	Percentage of total
Open employment	67	44
Unemployed†	65	43
Youth Opportunities Programme	9	4
Sheltered employment	6	6
Day Centre and Adult Training Centre	5	3
Voluntary Work	1	–

† Eleven people in this group were not seeking employment mainly because of family commitments or ill-health.

The situation over all: Looking at the situation over all in terms of occupation since leaving St Loye's, 66 per cent of the respondents had obtained open employment, although one third of them were no longer so employed. Eighteen per cent of people had not been involved in any form of structured activity. Nine per cent had been involved in YOPs, five per cent in sheltered work, five per cent in day centres or adult training centres and one per cent in voluntary work. The figures are detailed in Table 2.4. These percentages exceed 100 because a few people had been involved in more than one category and this will be expanded on by looking at each type of occupation in detail.

The figures in the table cannot be considered in isolation and the time in employment, the relation between employment and training, the type of employment and reasons for leaving employment are discussed elsewhere in this chapter. What is clear at this stage is that 34 per cent of the respondents had never obtained open employment and of those that had a substantial proportion had since left their work. It should also be appreciated that the picture is not static. The cut-off point for the collection of information was 31 October 1980, but a number of young people's situations changed after this point. Between filling in their questionnaires and being interviewed two young men had been made redundant and two more redundancies were identified through the employers' questionnaires. One young man has since left employment to attend a medical assessment centre, and one young woman who was classified as unemployed is now known to be in open employment. Another young man had been unemployed since leaving St Loye's but when interviewed was doing a course at an Employment Rehabilitation Centre.

Table 2.4: Occupation over all since leaving St Loye's

Occupation	Actual number involved	Percentage of total
Open employment	101	66
Unemployed	27	18
Youth Opportunities Programme	14	9
Sheltered Work	7	5
Day Centre	7	5
Voluntary Work	2	1

Open Employment

As has already been stated there were 101 people in this study who had obtained open employment since leaving St Loye's and this next section is concerned with the details of employment obtained. Respondents to the questionnaire were allowed space to give details of up to six jobs that they might have had since leaving St Loye's, though only one young man had had that many jobs. Sixty-two per cent had only had one job and 26 per cent had had two jobs. The percentage of time that each person had spent in open employment since leaving St Loye's was calculated with the exception of seven respondents who gave incomplete information. Of the 94 people for whom it was possible, 72 per cent had been in employment for over 50 per cent of their time since leaving St Loye's, and half of these had been for 90 per cent or more of the time. Twenty-one per cent of the young people had been employed for less than 30 per cent of the time. The percentage of time in open employment for the young people in this study did not differ significantly by year of leaving. The figures are given in Table 2.5.

Table 2.5: Percentage of time that the young people have been in open employment since leaving St Loye's (n = 94)

Percentage time in employment	Percentage of young people
0–10	9
11–20	5
21–30	7
31–40	2
41–50	5
51–60	1
61–70	10
71–80	9
81–90	16
91–100	36

It was not possible to calculate the length of time in their first job for eight people who had had open employment as they had omitted to provide accurate dates. Forty-two per cent of those who obtained open employment had been in their first job for less than six months. Rather less than half of these young people who had such short periods of employment were now unemployed, indeed for nearly a quarter of them (nine) that first short spell of open employment had been their only employment.

There were 39 young people who went into a first job that lasted for less than six months. Of those:

nine did not obtain further employment;

three had only recently left St Loye's;

12 had since had unstable work histories or had left open employment;

13 had had stable work histories (of whom two were currently unemployed);

two were in their first jobs which had taken them some time to find.

The nine who had had just one short period of employment had lost their jobs because of their seasonal nature, redundancy, unsuitable premises or sacking. Of those who had gone on to other work from a first short job, rather less than half (12) had an unstable employment history or had now left open employment. Two of them were now doing sheltered work and another two were on Youth Opportunities Programmes. The others had had further open employment though this had been short-term and sporadic and only one of them was currently employed. One young man, for example, had left St Loye's two and a half years ago and had since worked in a craft factory for six weeks, a laundry for four months, a garage for two weeks, a double-glazing firm for six weeks and a hotel for a week.

There were 13 young people who went on to have stable employment histories. One young man had managed to keep himself in employment for most of the three years since leaving St Loye's through a series of temporary jobs. He had trained in store-keeping and had held five jobs, four of them as a storeman. At the time of writing he had been unemployed for two months because the contract on his last job (which he had held for nearly a year) had run out. Another young man had had four jobs since leaving college three years ago and had kept himself in employment for 90 per cent of the time. He was now unemployed due to redundancy. The situation of these two young men and the others already mentioned above may worsen as they become older and their periods of unemployment lengthen.

Of these 13 young people who had gone on to have stable work histories several had progressed to a second placement in which they were still employed. Indeed four of them had left their first employment because they were able to take up a better position. One young man had left his first job as 'the work I was doing had nothing to do with what I was taught at St Loye's' and had for the last three and a half years been employed in work that allowed him to use his electronic wiring skills. Another young man had had five fairly short jobs (partly due to his moving house) but was now re-employed by the employers of his third job as 'I worked there before and they told me I could come back anytime'. There were also two young people who had only been in their first jobs for a matter of months as they had had to wait eight and 18 months respectively to find work.

A fairly stable first placement did not always result in a stable placement in employment over all. There was a group of young people whose first job had lasted for longer than six months but who were currently unemployed. The percentage of the time that these young people had been in employment since leaving St Loye's varied between 19 and 82 per cent with a mean of 47 per cent. The majority (six of them) had only one job placement and had left because of dissatisfaction with the work, being sacked or finding the taxi fares too expensive. The other young people had had two or more jobs following a fairly long first job. One young man had left a job as a semi-skilled assembly wirer because there was 'a better job going at the time, which had much better pay, plus I wanted to widen my experience'. The first job had lasted for 18 months and the second for only 6 months as it had been contract employment and he had not been kept on. In the two and a half years since leaving the second job he had had three other wiring jobs and further training. His speed of work seemed to be the reason for his leaving employment. For his third job he wrote 'I left because I couldn't cope with the work and my dad died at that time'. His initial move to a better position had had unfortunate consequences and at the time of this study he had been unemployed for seven months.

As has already been stated 36 per cent of the people who had had open employment had been so employed for over 90 per cent of the time since leaving St Loye's. All these young people were still in open employment – indeed two thirds of them were still in their first job. The majority of them had been employed for well over a year. Of the third who were in their second or subsequent job only one young man felt that his work performance had been a factor in his leaving his first job. The others had left employment largely because of redundancy or to obtain a better position.

The 101 young people who had had open employment had obtained 164 jobs between them. Sufficient detail was obtained on 161 of these jobs to classify them into occupational groupings taken from the Registrar General's listing of occupations. These groupings are listed in Table 2.6.

Respondents to the questionnaire were asked about their pay and the number of hours they worked. Details of take-home pay were available for 160 of the jobs obtained, with respondents being asked to indicate which of four groupings their weekly income came under. Taking the figures for all jobs obtained, 8 per cent of the jobs paid less than £20, 45 per cent between £20 and £40, 38 per cent between £40 and £60 and 9 per cent over £60. Looking at the current wages (October 1980) of those in open employment, all the young people

Table 2.6: Occupational Groupings (n = 161)

Occupation	Percentage of jobs obtained
Catering, cleaning and other personal services.	10
Processing, making, repairing and related occupations (metal and electrical)	16
Clerical and related occupations	35
Transport operating, materials moving and storing and related occupations	17
Professional and related occupations and science, engineering, technology and similar fields	2
Selling occupations	5
Making and repairing occupations excluding metal and electrical	5
Painting, repetitive assembling, product inspecting, packaging and relevant occupations	7
Gardening, fishing and related occupations	3

were earning more than £20. Thirty-six per cent were earning between £20 and £40 (one of these was working part-time), 48 per cent between £40 and £60 and 16 per cent over £60. For a substantial proportion of the young people financial difficulties are cushioned by living with their parents. For those whose earnings fall below £40 a week there can be no clear-cut financial incentive to work by comparison with supplementary benefit rates, particularly for those young people living independently. At the time of this study, for example, the supplementary benefit rate for a single person was either £18.30 or £23.70 (the long-term rate) which with an addition for housing costs of perhaps £15 a week and access to other welfare benefits, in cash or kind, would provide an income in excess of that of many of this group. This is not to suggest that benefit rates be revised downwards, but rather to indicate that for many young people incentives other than financial provide the motivation to seek employment.

Francis had recently obtained work as a packer and spoke of his delight at having found employment at last. After deducting £5 per week for bus fares, his take-home pay was £28. The rent for his bed-sit took half of this and in an attempt to increase the £14 a week he had to live on he had attempted to cycle the 16 miles to work and back. He has cerebral palsy that severely affects his legs and found the journey impossible. He works from 8am–5pm and has a lower income than he did when he was unemployed. This young man is entitled to a rent allowance that would substantially improve his income, but was unaware of its existence.

The number of hours worked was available for 161 of the jobs obtained. Seven per cent of the jobs had been for 30 hours or less a week and 76 per cent had been for 31 to 40 hours a week. The most common figure given was 40 hours a week which was given for 55 per cent of the jobs. 17 per cent of the jobs involved working for between 41 and 70 hours a week. Of those young people currently in open employment, eight were working for over 40 hours a week. One young man does a 50-hour week as a forecourt attendant for between £40 and £60 a week, another has a 60-hour week and takes home over £60.

Information collected from the young people about the type of schooling they had received and the disabilities they suffered was also considered in relation to open employment. Dividing the respondents into those who had attended ordinary school and those who had attended a special school or had had home tuition, it appears that those people who had attended ordinary school were rather more likely to have ever been in open employment. Seventy-two per cent of this group had obtained open employment whereas only 60 per cent of those from special education had done so. Young people with special needs attending ordinary school are likely to be less severely disabled than those attending special schools or receiving home tuition.

A breakdown of the young people in terms of their disabilities and open employment is provided in Table 2.7.

The figures in the Table suggest that those young people with the 'invisible' handicaps of hearing impairment or communication disorders and cardiac function impairment had obtained a fairly high proportion of jobs in open employment. Those people with epilepsy had a rather lower 'success' rate than might be expected following the 'invisible' handicap theme, and they may have to overcome considerable misunderstanding amongst the general public, which of course includes employers. This last point was made by the professionals

Table 2.7: Young people's disabilities and open employment

Disability	Young people	Obtained open employment	Currently in open employment
Upper limb	5	2	1
Lower limb	4	3	2
Paraplegia	4	1	1
Other spinal disabilities	5	4	3
Arthritis	3	1	1
Cardiac	9	8	3
Epilepsy	16	11	7
Hemiplegia	20	13	11
Hearing impaired and communication disorders	12	11	7
Cerebral Palsy	8	6	4
Muscular dystrophy	3	2	2
Spina bifida	16	8	7
Visual handicap	10	5	3
Alimentary	6	2	2
Arthrogryposis multiplex congenita	4	3	0
Diplegia	10	8	5
Other	18	13	8
Total	153	101	67

concerned with job placement who were contacted during this study.

Looking at the young people in terms of the functional aspects of their disabilities (i.e. the visibility of their handicap, its effect on their communication and mobility) some interesting trends emerge. The grouping of the functional aspects of people's handicaps is discussed fully at the beginning of this chapter. The figures for the three functional aspects of disability are provided in Table 2.8. The figures in brackets refer to the actual number of young people in each group.

Table 2.8: Functional aspects of disability and open employment

Visibility of handicap		Impairment of mobility		Impairment of communication	
Group	% obtained open employment	Group	% obtained open employment	Group	% obtained open employment
A (41)	78	A (59)	75	A (132)	65
B (85)	64	B (69)	65		
C (27)	56	C (25)	48	B (21)	71

The table indicates that young people whose handicap was more visible or whose mobility was more impaired were less likely to have obtained open employment. On the other hand those with communication problems tended to have had slightly more experience of open employment. These trends fail to reach statistical significance.

The same trends emerge with the functional aspects of disability in relation to the current placement position. The figures are given in Table 2.9.

Table 2.9: Functional aspects of disability and current open employment

Visibility of handicap		Impairment of mobility		Impairment of communication	
Group	% in open employment	Group	% in open employment	Group	% in open employment
A (41)	49	A (59)	51	A (132)	44
B (85)	47	B (69)	45		
C (27)	30	C (25)	28	B (21)	48

These differences do not reach statistical significance.

When the groupings for visibility of handicap and impairment of mobility were used to compare the total number of people currently in open employment, sheltered work or Youth Opportunities Programmes with those not so employed the difference in both cases reached statistical significance. For visibility $\chi^2 = 7.57$ with 2d.f. and for mobility $\chi^2 = 6.66$ with 2d.f. (both significant at the 5 per cent level). The difference in the communication scores does not reach statistical significance.

The relationship between the functional aspects of disability and open employment record is more apparent if those who have spent more than 90 per cent of their time in open employment are compared with those who have never held employment. The number of people in each group is given in Table 2.10.

Table 2.10: Functional aspects of disability, comparing those who have never worked with those who have been in open employment for more than 90 per cent of the time

	Visibility of handicap			Impairment of mobility			Impairment of communication	
Group	Non-workers	More than 90%	Group	Non-workers	More than 90%	Group	Non-workers	More than 90%
A	7	11	A	9	19	A	27	27
B	17	24	B	15	18			
C	12	4	C	12	2	B	9	12

Visibility $-\chi_0^2 = 5.97$ with 2d.f. (significant at the 5 per cent level)
Mobility $-\chi_0^2 = 10.88$ with 2d.f. (significant at the 1 per cent level)
Communication – not significant

These figures suggest that young people may be more disadvantaged in the labour market when their handicap affects their presentation to other people and their mobility. The concept of stigma is discussed in Chapter Five where it is suggested that a policy of public education combined with social and job-related skills training for the young people may alleviate some of this disadvantage. The physical problems imposed on those people with impaired mobility by the design of many buildings and means of transport are slowly coming to be recognized.

Reasons for leaving employment

All respondents to the questionnaire were asked why they had left their previous employment (if applicable) and the reasons were further discussed with those young people interviewed. There were 54 young people who provided at least one reason for leaving a job in open employment and between them they gave 96 answers. The most common reason given was redundancy, or job closure, and this accounted for 30 per cent of all answers. A third of the jobs that ended in redundancy were known to be lost either because of their seasonal nature or because the employers were cutting down on staff generally or closing down. For the other young people who were made redundant it is not known whether or not there were large scale redundancies as these respondents had not given detailed information. Rather more than half of the young people made redundant had not obtained further work whereas others had gone on to other jobs in which they were all now employed. There was one young man who had trained in electronic wiring, obtained a wiring job soon after leaving St Loye's and had been employed for eight months before being made redundant. He had soon found another job as an electronic production operator only to be made redundant again 17 months later.

There were only six people who wrote that they had been sacked and for most of them it was, they claimed, because their employers felt that their work was not fast enough. One young man had obtained work as a stock control clerk soon after leaving college and had been sacked eight months later as 'the job was too hard. I did not work quick enough and I got behind'. Five months later he was working again as a clerk and this lasted for four months only as he was 'not good enough'. His next job as an assembler lasted for six months after which time he was made redundant. At the time of this study he was unemployed. He had not done a training course at St Loye's and wished that the college had given him 'a general knowledge of what to expect if you can't get a job'. Perhaps, due to his lack of success as a clerk it had been suggested to him that he undertake some training and he felt that 'The Jobcentre are always trying to put me on a training course. There comes a time when you have had enough training'.

There were 15 reasons given for leaving a job that related specifically to the person's disability. One young woman was indignant at having been 'asked to leave' her work as a cashier by the manager of the branch of a national supermarket chain. She had recently moved to the area to get married and had worked in another branch of the chain for 14 months. She had cerebral palsy and had some difficulty in walking though this did not affect her ability to operate a till, which she had done for some time to her previous manager's satisfaction.

One young man with right-sided spasticity had left three of his five jobs as he was unable to 'handle the job physically'. They were jobs he had heard about from friends and relatives and certainly from his description seemed quite unsuitable for someone with his physical limitations. However, employment found by the professional services may not always suit the needs of disabled people. One young man had found a job in his training trade of book-keeping and accounts through his disablement resettlement officer and had had to leave after a few months as the building was unsuitable. He was unemployed for 20 months before finding that job and had been unemployed again for over two years at the time of this study.

Another young woman had found one job through her Jobcentre and had left as she was unable to work 'at the pace set by piece work rate due to my disability'. Another job from the Jobcentre had been 'too heavy, lots of lifting'. She suffered from a skin disease that particularly affected her hands. Another young woman who was visually handicapped had gone for a job from the Jobcentre, only to find that it was a 'badly advertised job, was advertised as audio typist for which I was trained and I had to do (i.e. type) badly handwritten work'. This young woman had left her job after three days and found another as a chambermaid in a hotel. This had only lasted a matter of weeks as she claimed, 'a drunk kept trying to make a pass at me and the management did nothing'. It may be that more consultation with the professionals employed in the job placement services could help to ensure that disabled people did not go for jobs for which they were physically unsuited. Such failure may be extremely disheartening. One young woman trained as a typist had obtained four clerical jobs, all of them short-term and had left because of 'too much stress' or an inability to cope with the work. More professional involvement to smooth the young person's entry to employment may also be beneficial. A young man who had trained in book-keeping and accounts had obtained a job as a junior clerk, through his specialist careers officer and had had to leave after a matter of weeks as 'I found the work difficult to cope with at the speed required and some manual tasks difficult to complete due to my disability'. Fortunately this young man was now successfully placed as a bank clerk, a post he has held for two and a half years.

There were nine young people who left for a job that was more demanding or was better paid. There were also some young people who had been dissatisfied with the work, perhaps because they felt they had been misled about it or because it didn't suit them. One young man who trained in store-keeping had left his work as a store-keeper mainly because 'the stores was a mess but I was not allowed any control'. Perhaps a valid criticism from someone who has spent several months being instructed in how a stores should be run. He is now employed as a toll-bridge keeper. Another young woman who had trained as a telephonist had obtained a job answering the tele-phone for a taxi firm. She had been bored and dissatisfied as 'I thought I would be busier'. She was currently employed as a tele-phonist receptionist with the fire brigade where her workload was much heavier. She was confined to a wheelchair but was able to reach all the necessary rooms as they were on the ground floor. A young man trained in horticulture at St Loye's had obtained a job as a gardener handyman after 12 months of unemployment. He left the job after a month because as he suggested 'When I apply for a gardener/ handyman I expect to do both'. Given the length and comprehensive-ness of the horticulture course at St Loye's perhaps his dissatisfaction is not surprising. The reasons for leaving open employment are detailed in Table 2.11.

Table 2.11: Reasons for leaving employment (n = 96)

	First job	Second job	Third job	Fourth job	Fifth job	Sixth job	Total	%
Redundancy or job closure	14	6	3	4	2	–	29	30
Disability Related	9	2	2	1	1	–	15	16
Promotion	7	1	1	–	–	–	9	9
Sacked	4	1	–	–	1	–	6	6
Dissatisfaction	15	8	4	1	–	–	28	29
Other	5	1	1	1	–	1	9	10

Youth Opportunities Programmes

There has been a significant rise in the number of places on Govern-ment schemes for unemployed young people in the last few years. The Holland Report (1977) suggested that a few thousand such places were available in the early 1970s and that by 1976/77 the number was 124,800. A Department of Education and Science Circular (10/77) predicted that over 230,000 young people would take part in such schemes annually and described the form the schemes should take, based on the recommendations of the Holland Report. The Youth Opportunities Programme (YOP) is divided into two main types of programme – Work Preparation Courses and Work Experience. Those taking part in the YOP may be involved for a minimum of two weeks (the employment induction course) through to a maximum of about a year (on project-based work experience, a training workshop scheme or community service). A major part of the YOP is on the Work Experience on Employers' Premises (WEEP) which lasts for about six months, and it is this part of the programme that was used by the young people in this study.

Young people have to have been unemployed for at least six weeks before being offered a place on a YOP and they are given an allowance from the Government of £23.50 a week (March 1981) while on the scheme. Initially the YOP appeared to have generated a good deal of enthusiasm among young people themselves and a current pamphlet by the Manpower Services Commission gives details of the YOP and suggests 'Your certificate and the experience and skills you'll pick up, will help you when you apply for jobs. Most people find they can get a job much more easily after they have been on a scheme'.

Such enthusiasm may have been warranted when the scheme began. The figure of 60 per cent had been quoted in relation to permanent job placements as a result of YOP placements (Turner, 1980) and the Secretary of State, Mr James Prior, has also claimed that nearly seven out of ten young people go straight into jobs from a YOP. These figures have since been challenged by the Institute of Careers Officers (*Times Educational Supplement*, 30.1.81) whose secretary, Mr Ray Hurst, said that he was convinced that such figures were out of date and suggested that 'In many parts of the country only one in five of the youngsters get jobs and nationally the proportion is probably now less than half of what Mr Prior is claiming'. Only one in three young people in North Tyneside who take part in the YOP get a job after finishing according to a recent study (Into Work research project, 1981).

Rowan (1980) suggested that the YOP was proving (after a year's experience) to be an important way of giving handicapped young people an introduction to working life if they are to settle in employment. It was also felt that WEEP 'has proved to be a very effective way into permanent employment for handicapped young people'. The more recent figures for placements coupled with the fact that disabled young people are more likely to be unemployed than their able-bodied peers suggest, however, that the effectiveness of the YOP for placing such young people in permanent employment may be limited. This was certainly the case in the present study. There were 14 young people known to have taken part in the YOP since leaving St Loye's and of the five people who had finished their YOP all were now unemployed including one young person who had initially been kept on. One young man with mild cerebral palsy spent five terms in the Further Education Unit and then took a 52-week comprehensive and practical course in horticulture. Since leaving the College he has been involved in two schemes, one as a general gardener and one as a labourer. In neither case was he offered employment beyond the duration of the scheme. He had been unemployed for six months when this information was collected and was concerned that he was not having a chance to further his experience. At the time of his interview another young man was concerned about whether he would be kept on by the firm when his second six-month period of work experience ran out. As his mother suggested, 'You'd think they'd know by now whether or not they wanted him!' The questionnaire returned from his employer was positive and affirmed that this young man had given a fair day's work but also stated that he had ceased to be employed by them when his work experience period had come to an end. Another young man doing WEEP classified himself as not working and wrote of 'A feeling of rejection and frustration, having very little money. A feeling of being used as cheap labour attributed work experience'. His last point was of concern to Colin Barnett, Chairman of the Manpower Services Commission, Lancashire and Manchester, and Regional Secretary of the TUC, who suggested in a recent article, that if teenagers are paid £23.50 a week 'it becomes the going rate'. He further comments that some of the employers he deals with in connection with the YOP feel that the scheme is exploitative.

Clearly there is concern about the role of the YOP and whatever else young people may gain from participation, many will undoubtedly be unemployed afterwards. One young woman in this study asked why she had left her job had written 'My time was up. It was only a six-month course'. A recent report (Youth A.I.D. (1981)) suggested in the light of trends discussed above, that the YOP should be relaunched as a twelve-month programme of further education and preparation for work, because the present programme will not be able to take the strain of increasing youth unemployment. With the MSC predicting school leaver unemployment of 80 per cent a YOP espoused as a way of getting young people jobs will surely lose credibility.

Sheltered Employment

Sheltered employment is intended to be for disabled people who are not able to work in open employment but are nevertheless capable of productive work. The generally stated minimum requirement for admission is the ability to work at one-third of the normal rate. Sheltered work is provided in three different ways:

1. By Remploy Limited, a public company that has almost ninety sheltered workshops and factories throughout the country;
2. By local authorities. Social Service Departments are required to provide sheltered workshops for disabled people;
3. By voluntary bodies. These may cater for people with specific handicaps or may be attached to specialist colleges.

Remploy employees work a 40-hour week, producing leather and textile goods or furniture or being involved in packaging or assembly. Their wages are based on a standard minimum Remploy rate agreed with the trade unions. Remploy sheltered workshops are the main providers of sheltered work for disabled people, providing about two-thirds of over 12,000 places. The company is heavily subsidized by the Government and needs to reduce its financial deficit. As Greaves and Massie (1977) suggest such a need for profitability may mean that Remploy are only taking employees with minor disabilities.

Admission to sheltered employment is administered by the disablement resettlement officer who has to decide whether or not a person is capable of open employment – a decision that may have implications for a person's whole working life. Remploy do not see their role as one of rehabilitation. A young man who suffered from a severe hearing loss had completed a 26-week joinery course at St Loye's and he eventually obtained open employment as a bench joiner. He was only employed for a month as 'They thought I was a fully qualified craftsman. I was not therefore suitable for the job'. This ex-trainee is now working, also as a bench-joiner, in a Remploy factory and finds that he 'likes the kind of work'. If, as Greaves and Massie (op. cit.) suggest 'Usually if a disabled person enters a sheltered workshop he can say goodbye to open employment', then young people such as the one above may be inappropriately placed.

One young woman had worked in a sheltered workshop for a brief period until 'they ran out of work for me to do' and she is now unemployed. Of the six young men currently in sheltered work, four were employed by Remploy, one by the local authority and one by a voluntary body. Graham has spina bifida and is handicapped to the extent that he feels 'my only problem is that it's difficult for me to find shirts to fit and I can't wear a tie'. He trained as an electronic wireman at St Loye's but did not complete the course. After applying unsuccessfully for several jobs in open employment he obtained work in the local Workshop for the Blind, where he is pleased to be allocated to the woodwork section as he 'couldn't stick making buttons'. During his six months of unemployment he was turned down for work on medical grounds as it was felt that he wouldn't be able to lift goods, a rejection that he now finds ironic as lifting is a regular part of his present work.

Another young man who did not complete his electronic wiring course is now working in a sheltered workshop attached to a hospital where he enjoys his work, because 'although it is sometimes repetitive, it is mainly quite varied and I find it quite satisfying to be involved in construction and finishing products'. This young man's work as a machinist/bench operator is far more interesting and less repetitive than he expected. Another ex-trainee was now employed as a packer in a Remploy factory and was dissatisfied with his work, claiming that 'It was not what I had expected to do when I went to work there'. Another young man who had completed his training at St Loye's felt that his general factory work was 'better money than the DHSS (his Supplementary Benefit) and you do not sit around doing nothing', but felt concern at having trained as a storekeeper, applied for stores work and yet ended up on the shop floor. He had been unemployed for two and a half years before starting at the sheltered workshop.

His comments perhaps indicate the dilemma of those young people who have been to St Loye's and who are employed in sheltered work. They have been to a college where open employment has been held out as the goal, with sheltered employment a poor alternative. Five of the seven people who had had sheltered employment had had vocational training at St Loye's (only three had completed it) and for those young people there may well have been a sense of settling for less. Sheltered employment may provide a valuable opportunity for those unable to manage open employment but capable of productive work because it provides access to the psychological and social benefits of employment. Heavy Government subsidies make the employment of severely disabled people possible in sheltered workshops and such work is considered by many people to provide dignity and to be worth the expense. It is important however that this role is maintained in the face of possible pressures to employ less severely disabled people displaced from the open employment market.

Day Centres and Adult Training Centres

Day centres and adult training centres (ATCs) were attended by a small number of the people in this study. Such centres are usually provided through Local Authority Social Services, and are designed for disabled people who, it is felt, are unable to work in sheltered or open employment. Activities are provided to occupy those attending and the staff in ATCs may feel that training is one of their objectives. The centres may serve a useful social function and do at least get disabled people out of their homes. People attending centres are not paid a wage but may receive a small allowance. One young man had attended a day centre one day a week and had received 50p for it. Another young woman was given £3.25 for a five-day week at an ATC.

The young man already mentioned raised a crucial issue when asked why he had left the centre as he stated '. . . there were mixed handicapped people (mentally handicapped) and I couldn't stick there any longer'. This young man had been unemployed in the four years since leaving St Loye's and had not taken part in any structured activity apart from his spell at the day centre. In the Warnock Report (1978) (15.47) it was recommended that 'arrangements for the education and training of young adults in adult training centres and day centres should be separate from those for older people, since it may be possible for the young people to make considerable progress if a special programme is developed for them'. The Report was concerned with the inappropriateness of present provisions but it is interesting to

note that whereas Warnock referred to ATCs for mentally handicapped people and day centres for physically handicapped people,
five people in this study who were physically handicapped were
attending ATCs.

One young woman who was partially-sighted had successfully
completed a six-month cookery course at St Loye's and in the three
and a half years since leaving the College had been unemployed apart
from attending a local day centre. Her mother added a post-script to
the questionnaire explaining the anger and frustration she had felt
since her daughter had left St Loye's, saying that 'All the people she
has seen say what they would like for Sally but nothing ever comes of
it'. She added, 'Sally feels rejected and as a family it is tearing us
apart, she attends a day centre for five days a week. It is not the place
for her, but what else is there for her to do'. It is perhaps illustrative of
the position of disabled young people in centres that only three
parents added to the questionnaire sent out to the young people and
all three were commenting on day centres and ATCs.

Only two of the five people attending centres classified themselves
as working. It is of interest that both these young people are living in
hostels near their centres and have to a large extent established their
independence. The mother of one of them felt that her daughter has a
full-time occupation with considerable job-satisfaction on the whole,
but added 'She would probably not be at the ATC if there were a more
suitable opportunity for her. . .'. Her daughter expressed satisfaction
with her work as she enjoyed 'making things like soft toys, trays,
stools, aprons, bags, etc' and seemed to cope with what her mother
described as a 'pioneer project in the country' in terms of accommodation and everyday living.

Some young people may benefit from attendance at a day centre or
ATC and hostel accommodation, if widely enough available, could
provide them with an opportunity to achieve independence. However, attendance at such a centre is not a successful placement in the
sense that open employment is. It would be seen by most people
involved as a step down. The line between encouraging people
enough so that their potential for open employment is maximized, but
not so much that they feel personal failure if they do not attain it is an
extremely difficult one to draw. One young man attending a day
centre, was asked about what changes he would make to the Further
Education Unit wrote 'more talks about the actual employment
you're likely to get'.

Voluntary Work

There were two young women taking part in this study who had undertaken voluntary work. Neither of them had obtained open employment, although one had turned down a job that she felt to be unsuitable. She is confined to a wheelchair and had worked in the kitchen of an old people's home. The other young woman trained as a typist at St Loye's and was doing secretarial duties in a local hospital. She had been unemployed in the five years since leaving College and was no longer seeking employment as she and her husband wanted to start a family. She enjoyed her voluntary work and felt that it helped to relieve the boredom of being at home all day.

Training Courses and their Relation to Employment

As was stated earlier 70 per cent of the young people who took part in this study went on from the Further Education Unit to do a training course at the College. Details of the course were given in the Introduction and these young people participated in 11 of the courses available. An analysis of the ex-trainees' work experiences and the training they received suggests trends which may be of interest although the numbers in the individual categories are very small.

There were 55 respondents who had taken a commercial course and 53 who had had a technical training. Over all, 67 per cent of those with a commercial background had obtained open employment and in nearly every case this was related to their training trade. Seventy-four per cent of those with technical training had obtained open employment of whom only about two-thirds had obtained jobs related to their training course. Those people who had had more than one job were classified as having had related open employment if at least one of their jobs had been related to their training course. This discussion is summarized in Table 2.12.

Thus while people with a technical training were slightly more likely to obtain open employment than those with a commercial training, having obtained employment the latter group were more likely to be in work that was related to their training trade. This difference in obtaining related open employment reached statistical significance ($\chi^2 = 6.92$ significant at the one per cent level). A breakdown of placements in terms of each training is given in Table 2.13. The figures refer to the actual number of young people in each category.

Table 2.12: Respondent's training trade and its relation to employment

	Obtained open employment		Obtained related open employment	
	Actual number	Percentage	Actual number	Percentage
Commercial training n = 55	37	67	34	92
Technical training n = 53	39	74	25	64
No training course n = 45	25	56	–	–

Table 2.13: Open Employment and Training Courses

Course	Number taking course	Obtained open employment	Obtained related open employment	Currently in open employment	Currently in related open employment
Technical Courses					
Store-keeping	20	14	11	10	6
Horticulture	8	5	2	0	0
Cookery	3	2	1	2	1
Joinery	3	3	3	2	2
Light electro-mechanical fitting	6	5	2	4	2
Electronic wiring	13	10	6	5	3
Commercial Courses					
Data preparation	8	6	6	5	5
General clerical	1	1	1	1	1
Copy, audio or shorthand typing	8	5	5	2	2
Book-keeping and Accounts	17	12	12	6	6
Telephonist/Typing	21	13	10	10	6

Of the young people currently in open employment 30 per cent (i.e. 20 respondents) had not done a training course at the College, 51 per cent were in open employment related to their training trade and 19 per cent were employed in work unrelated to their training trade. These figures are similar to those for all those who have had open employment since leaving the College. Twenty-five per cent of the young people who had obtained open employment had not done a training course at the College, 58 per cent had obtained open employment that was related to their training trade and 17 per cent employment unrelated to their training.

It is important to look at the figures above in more detail. For example, of the 13 people trained in telephony and typing who had obtained open employment, 10 had been employed for over 70 per cent of their time since leaving St Loye's. The other three had been in employment for less than 30 per cent of the time. Two who had been in employment for 96 and 89 per cent of the time since leaving College respectively were employed in work unrelated to telephony and typing. Of four people who did not complete the training two had been in employment for most of the time since leaving (89 and 88 per cent respectively), one had never worked and one had been employed for less than a month before being asked to leave. This will indicate the difficulty in interpreting measures of 'successful' employment experiences.

There were 12 people trained in book-keeping and accounts who had obtained open employment. Of the ten who provided accurate employment histories only three had been in employment for over 70 per cent of the time since leaving College and, indeed, five had been employed for less than 30 per cent of the time. Two of these young people were currently in employment though one had been unemployed for a considerable time as he had found his first job unsuitable and had wanted more varied work where he could use his training. Another had left the course a few weeks early because she was felt to have trained 'to the limit of her capacity' on the St Loye's course and had then gone on to a local MSC Data Processing course. She is currently employed as an accounts clerk – a post she enjoys. Another young woman had been employed as a clerk for nine months but had left, she suggested because 'I did not expect to have to start the book-keeping from scratch. Also I was made to understand that I would be working full-time within a few months of starting the job. This did not happen'. Another young woman had been made redundant and one young man had left over a dispute with his employer about his eligibility for a written contract of employment.

Of the six young men who had taken the light electro-mechanical fitting course, two had obtained related open employment. One of them had been in the same job for 89 per cent of the time since leaving College but was dissatisfied 'Because I feel that what I know, I am not putting to full use. I also feel that I am in a dead-end job'. Three other people who had obtained open employment had all been employed for at least 60 per cent of the time since leaving College, indeed two of them were currently in employment. A young man who had left the course just less than half way through is at present unemployed, though he has kept himself in employment for 75 per cent of the time through a series of short-term unskilled jobs.

Of the five young women who had trained as typists and obtained open employment only two were so employed at the moment and four had been in employment for less than 20 per cent of their time since leaving College. One of these had had to wait eight months for a job, but she was pleased because it was 'What I wanted'. The other young woman in employment was in a temporary job and had had three other jobs since leaving the College. These had been short-term posts and she had left because of 'too much stress' or being 'unable to cope with the work'. Another young woman is presently on a YOP placement having had two other jobs since leaving College, one having been left through redundancy and the other because 'they really wanted some-body with better qualifications'.

Of the 45 young people who had not taken a training course 56 per cent had obtained open employment and all but one of these were still so employed. Accurate employment histories were available for 22 of these young people and 16 of them had been in open employment for over 80 per cent of their time since leaving St Loye's.

The percentage of time that young people had been in open employment since leaving St Loye's is given in Table 2.14 with the exception of seven young people who did not provide complete enough information. Separate figures are given for young people who did not do a training course, those who did a commercial course and those who did a technical course. The percentages and the actual number of young people are given.

Looking at those people who had done a training course, those with a technical training were more likely to have been in open employment for over 80 per cent of their time since leaving St Loye's. This reached statistical significance ($x^2 = 6.02$ significant at the 2 per cent level). Those people who did not do a training course are also more likely than commercial-course trainees to have been in employment for over 80 per cent of the time, and so taking the three groups the distribution is significant at the 5 per cent level ($\chi^2 = 6.39$ with 2d.f.).

Table 2.14: Open Employment and Training

Percentage of time in open employment	No training course (n = 42)		Commercial training (n = 53)		Technical training (n = 51)	
0	47.6	20	33.9	18	27.4	14
1–10	2.4	1	11.3	6	2.0	1
11–20	2.4	1	5.7	3	2.0	1
21–30	0.0	0	9.4	5	3.9	2
31–40	0.0	0	1.9	1	2.0	1
41–50	2.4	1	0.0	0	7.8	4
51–60	2.4	1	0.0	0	0.0	0
61–70	2.4	1	5.7	3	9.8	5
71–80	2.4	1	11.3	6	2.0	1
81–90	9.5	4	5.7	3	15.7	8
91–100	28.6	12	15.1	8	27.4	14

Seventeen per cent of the trainees who commenced a training course did not complete it, mainly because the college staff did not feel that they could benefit any further from training. However 67 per cent of the young people who had not completed a training course went on to obtain open employment. Such premature departures may be disheartening for the young people concerned and given that many do go on to obtain open employment there may be merit in reconsidering such measures.

The sex distribution of young people on the training courses revealed that women very rarely undertook training for traditionally male occupations. None of them trained in store-keeping, joinery, light electro-mechanical fitting or horticulture and only one young woman trained in electronic wiring and one took the catering course. The same pattern emerged in the more traditionally female commercial sector in that no young men were involved in typing, Data Preparation or general clerical courses. However, there were five young men on telephony courses and 12 on the book-keeping and accounts course. A booklet giving details of the training courses available at St

Loye's points out the desirability of young women considering manual skills training. Young men and women might usefully consider the full range of courses available.

Difficulties at work

The questionnaire gave respondents an opportunity to note any difficulties they may have had at work because of their disability. There were 39 people who wrote that they had encountered such difficulty. Nine of them reported that the physical exertion required in their work created a problem sometimes. Some comments were:

'I have problems lifting heavy objects because of my weak arms but they (colleagues) are very good and helpful';
'I have had small problems, like my hips or backache from standing up for long periods';
'I had trouble with my knees which made it quite painful with all the lifting'.

The majority of responses (24) suggested difficulties that were not concerned with the content of the work but with related issues such as mobility and communication. One young woman wrote 'transport is the main difficulty because I cannot get on and off public transport'. Another that 'Well, the Ladies was a bit difficult for a wheelchair so they had it altered for me and another girl in a chair, they also had metal sheets put on the bottom of the doors, they are very helpful and would do anything that would make things easier'. One young man with aphasia wrote that he had 'Difficulty in understanding all instructions' and also that he was not used to 'leg-pulling from other employees'. Kevin who has a hearing impairment stated that 'I don't always hear what people say. I don't always understand what people want. Most people are helpful and explain what they want'. Other related issues included the young man who wrote that he had difficulty with 'certain tasks such as folding items for insertion into envelopes and tying parcels and also carrying trays of coffee up and down stairs and through doors.' Another young man had had 'a few days off because of an asthma attack'.

The other six responses indicated general problems such as 'I was late for work a few times due to my taxi being late, therefore I missed out on pay because of it' and 'I was treated very protectively and felt as if I was wasting my time as I was not allowed any further opportunities which eventually made the job rather boring'. This last point was also made by one young man interviewed who felt that his no doubt well-meaning colleagues had fussed over him like 'mother hens'.

It seems clear that some disabled young people are confronted by physical difficulties at work directly related to their handicap and in some cases this leads to their leaving employment. In the majority of cases difficulties did not reflect an intrinsic incompatibility between the young person and their job and they could probably have been surmounted by changes in the job content or environment. The balance between disregarding the implications of a handicap and being over-protective is difficult to achieve. This is illustrated by Christine's two experiences of employment. In her first job as a keypunch operator her supervision and clarity of instruction did not make due allowance for her aphasia and after a brief trial she was asked to leave. At the start of her second job, however, a friend from the local club for the deaf accompanied Christine and he was able to interpret the job requirements to her. Two years later she was still successfully employed in a post as demanding as the first one.

The Employers' Questionnaire

As was stated in the Introduction, the 56 employers whose employees gave their consent were contacted and a response rate of 84 per cent meant that information was available from 47 employers. Forty three of these were ordinary open employment posts and four were part of the Youth Opportunities Programme. The term employers is used, although for many of these people the questionnaire would have been completed by a supervisory colleague.

The comments made by the employers were overwhelmingly positive as regards the employment performance of the young people. Eighty-one per cent of employers felt that they got a 'fair day's work' from their particular employee as compared to their able-bodied workers. Of the remaining employers three were unable to decide on an answer either way and most of those with a definite negative answer qualified it. One 'don't know' employer felt that although most of the able-bodied employees are very flexible and can be moved whenever required for whatever purpose there are limitations for a disabled person. Obviously this only applies to certain categories of disability and this employer did state that 'for specialised jobs though, no complaints'. Another employer felt that whether or not this employee gave a fair day's work 'depends on the day' – a comment which could surely be applied to many people, able-bodied and disabled alike. In a sense this section is unfair in that it is putting the work performance of this group of young people under scrutiny in a way that is rarely, if ever, done for able-bodied members of society. There is no 'norm' to relate these findings to. One employer felt that his employee did not give a fair day's work and added 'But he does try hard and is very personable'. Another young man has restricted mobility and according to his employer, 'Paul's disability makes him slower to look up entries from our debit note files, also slower to actually file work and check records'. The employer is, however, 'prepared to accept this'.

Employers were asked about their young worker in terms of any accidents they may have had, any extra time off they may have taken and about the effect (if any) the person's disability has on his or her work. These were considered to be the areas of concern to the employers and potential employers of disabled people. There were seven people who had had an accident at work, and these were mostly accidents related to the type of work they were doing. One young man who is a sheet metal worker had suffered some 'minor cuts as (had) all other operators'. Another working as an agricultural labourer had 'had a few days off work and we understand that he strained his back slightly, but recovered quickly'. One young woman who had restricted mobility had apparently had occasional 'tumbles'. Another young woman who suffers from epilepsy had had some convulsions at work and 'on the few occasions we have not been able (to help her) she has fallen and knocked herself'.

There were seven people whom their employers considered to have had more time off with illness than other employees. Two of their employers qualified their answers with 'but marginal' and 'possibly a little as she has migraine'. One employer of a young woman who had not had extra time off added 'Sick Record *nil*' to this answer, and another added to his answer that the attendance of disabled people was, in his experience, 'exemplary'. Fifteen of the employers felt that their worker's disability did affect his or her work, though for most people any difficulties were minimal. One young man whose strength was limited was 'unable to lift heavy weights, i.e. stores, meats, etc' in his work as a catering assistant. Another young man, similarly disabled, was said to have some difficulty lifting and carrying boxes, 'but this is by no means a major problem'. Another young man who had difficulty walking, was said to be affected in his work in 'a limited aspect of his slow mobility only'. A young woman, similarly disabled, was said to be affected by her disability 'not extensively, but even as an office worker the need arises for employees to be mobile, i.e. for running messages, going to the print room, filing etc'. One hearing-impaired young woman was said to have 'tantrums' due to her 'frustration at not being able to communicate as rapidly as those in her working group' and because 'she is a young girl and somewhat spoilt – we treat her like any other'.

One young man was employed as a storeman and his employer felt that 'John's disability does affect his speed of work, but the efficiency with which he carries out the paper work side more than compensates'. There were two employers who commented on the application of their employees to the work. One felt that his employee – a computer operator – showed a 'slight deterioration of concentration towards the end of the day'. Again it is obvious that such a comment could not be taken to imply a distinction between disabled and able-bodied workers. One employee was considered to be unable to work alone in his job as a labeller and his 'accuracy has to be checked by another employee'. Another young woman was described as '. . . although more than capable of handling equipment (as a telephonist) she tended to hit peaks and troughs of elation and depression at a high velocity'. Another young man, unusual in that his epilepsy was not well controlled, had had convulsions at work and was now resident at a medical assessment centre. Only one employee was considered by her employer to have difficulty in all three aspects of work performance, i.e. accidents, extra time off and disability-related limitations.

Employers were also asked about the placement of their employee and why they had decided to employ him or her. A careers officer or a disablement resettlement officer was said to be involved in 45 per cent of the placings, although it is possible that many employers were in fact referring to their contact with the Jobcentre. Where contact had been made with professional placement services all but one of the employers felt that a realistic assessment of the employee's suitability for the job had been made. The employer who did not, felt that it was very difficult to assess how an ex-trainee would develop in a commercial setting from his or her performance on a college course.

Nine employers specifically wrote of the personal qualities of their employees that had made them decide to engage them. One young woman has a 'hole in the heart' and her employer stated that he 'liked her courage and thought she deserved a chance'. Another young man 'appeared to be bright, open, honest, and determined' and another '. . . appeared friendly, good natured and was enthusiastic. He also applied for the job on his own initiative'. One employer's comment on the young man employed as an accounts clerk seems to be worth quoting at length.

> *Ken had gained good relevant qualifications in book-keeping, mathematics and accounting. His educational record at Chailey Heritage and St Loye's College illustrated his ability and conscientious interest in a commercial career. He seemed a pleasant, alert, determined young man interested in taking professional qualifications and training for a responsible position. Ken's disability did not influence our decision as to whether to employ or reject. Although he uses crutches, he moves with considerable agility and was clearly capable of participating fully in all aspects of office work and procedure.*

Another young man was described thus – 'He seemed capable – he was keen to find work. We thought he needed help'. He was engaged on a Youth Opportunities Programme and was found to be a 'good timekeeper, a willing worker, a pleasant person and of an independent and generally resourceful nature'. He was thought to have done a good day's work and to have benefited personally from his employment. At the time of writing his YOP had ended and he was unemployed.

Other employers commented that the attainments of their employees had been a factor in their decision to engage them. One young woman had done the work preparation course at St Loye's and then obtained work as a wirewoman. Her employer felt that she 'met the needs of the job' and that he had employed her 'to give her the opportunity to put her training into practice'. Another young woman employed as a book-keeping clerk was said to have been employed as she 'was suitably qualified and had relevant experience'. One employer wrote 'During the introductory period Susan proved to be a suitable Data Preparation Terminal Operator, and a vacancy existed'.

A few employers specifically made reference to the employment of disabled people when asked why they had decided to employ a particular person. One suggested that 'Everybody deserves a chance and providing they can perform their duties to the satisfaction of the employer, their disablement is irrelevant'. This employer added 'In our view they are more appreciative of having employment than most able-bodied personnel'. Another employer stated that the employee had the qualifications necessary and that 'we were trying to bring our numbers of disabled to correct proportion'. One employer who has 50 employees of whom five are disabled wrote 'We have a policy of employing disabled people in situations which are permanent and where their disability does not affect their performance when compared with able-bodied people'. Several employers when asked in general terms about their employment of disabled people answered the question in a way that was not readily quantifiable, for example 'All types of disabled people are employed by this department'. From those employers who did give figures it seems likely that of those for whom the quota system was applicable the majority were below the quota figure of three per cent.

The comments of two employers illustrate the extra demands made on disabled employees as they may have to surmount assumptions made about the abilities of 'the disabled' and have to prove themselves in a way beyond that normally expected of able-bodied people. One employer wrote 'For the young physically handicapped person there would seem to be particular problems in so far as, from an employer's viewpoint it is the range of 'low level' duties they can undertake which would get them employment in the first instance' and another that 'The disabled we feel must prove their own case, being honest with their problems, but also ready with their answers.'

There were five employers who had previously employed people with the same disability as the young person in question and two who had known such people. In the latter grouping one employer had a friend whose son had epilepsy and another had been involved in the rehabilitation of disabled people. Knowledge of other disabled people may certainly influence an employer, particularly if that knowledge is of 'good' disabled workers. One employer of a hearing-impaired young man noted that 'we already had a deaf and dumb employee doing the particular job (machine operator) and experienced no insurmountable difficulty. The two men in question made company for one another'.

Of those who would not consider such a placing one felt that she would consider employing a similarly disabled person in the future 'on work experience (part of the Youth Opportunities Programme) but not as a permanent member of the staff'. Such a comment suggests that the young man will not be offered permanent employment at the end of his placement and adds to the comments made about the scheme elsewhere in this chapter. Another employer already mentioned who had had an employee with epilepsy would not consider another similarly disabled person. This young man had epilepsy that was not controlled and had left work to have a medical assessment. West (1981) reports on the 'mistaken conceptions about epilepsy derived from hearsay, media reports and even implicit in language itself' and it may be that people who are uninformed see one disabled person as representative of others. Where their experience is a negative one this may have unfortunate consequences.

The questionnaire sent to employers provided some interesting material to supplement information collected from the young people themselves. The number of employers taking part was small but nevertheless the answers and comments received are valuable. Several employers used the space provided on the back of the questionnaire to make additional comments and in all but one instance these were positive. Two employers wrote that their employees had taken some time to settle into work and one of them stated 'After an initial three months she settled down and is now regarded as one of our better camera operators, with her work output matching that of her fellow operatives'. Alan's 'cheerful personality' was felt to assist him to overcome his disability and he was described as a conscientious hard-working employee who accepts responsibility and is respected by his colleagues. Nina's employers are impressed by her, her attitude to the job and her keenness though it is their impression 'that this is more to do with Nina as a person than with anything relevant to her disability'. The one negative comment spoke of one young man's personal cleanliness leaving much to be desired adding that 'he has had a formal warning for this'. The positive attitudes of employers of disabled people in this study add to the evidence collected by Kettle (1979b) in his review of research into the performance of disabled people at work. Clearly, given the opportunity many disabled people are able to work to their employer's satisfaction and to use their abilities.

Some points discussed in this chapter are given below.

- Less than half of the young people were currently in open employment although two-thirds of them had obtained such work since leaving St Loye's.

- Of those people who obtained open employment 62 per cent had only had one job and 26 per cent had had two jobs. Seventy-two per cent had been in employment for over 50 per cent of the time, indeed 36 per cent had been employed for over 90 per cent of the time.

- A first placement was not necessarily a crucial determinant of future placements in that some young people with short initial placements went on to have stable work histories and a stable first placement did not always result in a stable placement in employment over all.

- For a third of the young people the wages earned suggested that there were incentives other than financial that led them to obtain work.

- Some interesting trends emerged from a comparison of the young people who had obtained open employment in that those young people whose handicap affected their presentation to other people and their mobility were less likely to have obtained open employment or to be currently so employed.

- There were a substantial number of people who having obtained open employment or indeed skill-related open employment, had subsequently left it. The reasons for leaving are detailed at the end of the section on open employment. Clearly the main reason why people left employment – redundancy or job closure – reflects wider political and economic issues. The number of young people who wrote that they had been sacked was extremely small and corresponds with the comments of employers discussed earlier in this chapter. A substantial minority (45 per cent) left work for reasons that related to their disability or because they were dissatisfied with the work. More efficient job placings may counter at least some of this trend.

- The Youth Opportunities Programme had not proved to be a way into permanent employment for the small number of young people who had been involved. In the light of rising levels of youth unemployment the direction of the YOP may need rethinking.

- The employment of the few young men in sheltered work was discussed and the need for appropriate placing was stressed.

- There were five young people attending adult training centres although this provision is generally considered to be suitable for mentally handicapped people. There would seem to be a need for more appropriate provision for young physically handicapped people with hostel accommodation if required.

- Over all 70 per cent of the young people who took a training course had obtained open employment. Those with a commercial training were more likely to obtain work that was related to their training trade.

- Of those young people who had not taken a training course 56 per cent had obtained open employment and 72 per cent of these had been employed for more than 80 per cent of the time.

- Of the young people who had not completed the course, a majority (67 per cent) had obtained open employment. Offering these young people a modified course may be beneficial.

- A large minority of young people (45 per cent) did not however obtain open employment that was related to their training trade. At the time of this study, 51 per cent of young people in open employment were in jobs related to their training trade. There may well be merit in extending the training curriculum to include the job-related skills proposed by some of the respondents and discussed in Chapter Six. The FEU curriculum development discussed in Chapter Three may provide realistic alternatives. Clearly the relevance of a specific training lessens the longer a person is unemployed. The young people interviewed in this study who were unemployed were in the main looking for any work even though they may have wanted to work in their training trade when they left St Loye's.

- The difficulties that young people reported at work were in many cases surmountable by changes in the job content or environment or by providing support at the appropriate time.

- The comments made by the present employers of the young people were overwhelmingly positive. Eighty-one per cent felt that they got a fair day's work from their employee and 85 per cent that they would, in view of their experience, consider employing a similarly disabled person in the future.

- The young people had good work records in terms of accidents at work and extra time off with illness. Of those employees whose disability was said to affect their work, the restriction was minimal in most cases.

- Only eight employers felt that their employee's work had not been as good as they expected and of the others, over half felt that it was better. Employers wrote of the personal qualities and attainments that had made them decide to engage their employee and a few specifically made reference to the employment of disabled people.

CHAPTER THREE

The Significance of Work

This chapter is about the meaning of having employment. The satisfactions of those young people currently in employment, the work
aspirations of those interviewed and the situation of those unemployed are discussed. In the Warnock Report (op.cit.) there is a
short section termed 'Significant Living without Work' that is concerned with those people for whom paid employment is not a very real
possibility. It is suggested that 'working gives people a sense of
purpose and competence; it makes them feel needed; it provides a
change of environment so that they may appreciate their home better
when they return to it in the evening; it brings them into contact with
a different range of people from their friends at home and may lead to
fresh interests and social activities and it provides them with a
framework for the day and a routine which may help them to develop
self-discipline'.

Satisfactions

The young people answering the questionnaire who were currently in
employment were asked whether or not they were satisfied with their
work and were then asked why that was. Only four people did not
answer this question. Of the six people in sheltered work, four stated
that they were satisfied and some of their comments were discussed in
Chapter Two. One of the young men who was dissatisfied with his
work spoke of the problems when interviewed. He has spina bifida
and is currently employed in a Workshop for the Blind. He felt that

'the money's no good, you can't get promoted, the name dogs you and the name of the place frightens people. It's just like a small normal factory, but people ask you if you still make baskets there'. Of the seven people currently on YOPs who answered this question, five felt themselves to be satisfied with their work.

They commented on friendly workmates and interesting work. As one young man on his second work experience placement wrote, 'The reason why I am satisfied with my job that I am doing at the moment is because I can do the things that I am told to do and also I like the people I work with'. Of those not satisfied, one commented on the type of work he had to do and another on the fact that it was only a work experience scheme.

Sixty-five young people in open employment answered this question and only six of them were dissatisfied with the work they were doing. Most of these six wrote of the boredom of their work, and one felt that he 'would like more scope'. One young woman employed as a telephonist/receptionist wrote '. . . there is no kind of prospects of becoming a higher grade in the future, the money is not too good. . .'. Another young telephonist wrote, 'It is rather boring, not very stimulating at the best of times. I think I'm capable of something a bit more involved.'

Of those people who were satisfied with the work, the most frequently given reasons related to the content of the work. One young woman wrote, 'I like electrical wiring work and making things rather than office work' and a young bank clerk felt that 'I enjoy dealing with people and being part of a team and my job requires both of these things'. Several people combined a comment about the work content with one about the people they worked with. One young woman employed as a canteen assistant likes the people she works with and is 'never bored'. For another young woman 'The work is the kind I enjoy doing and all the people I work with are friendly'. One young woman, who has epilepsy, felt that 'the people I work with at present are very helpful and kind and are understanding about my disability'.

Only two young people mentioned money as a satisfaction of their work. A few were satisfied because it meant employment. One young man wrote 'I am fortunate to have a job when many able-bodied people haven't, so I feel it's one "up" for us disabled'. He added 'Also the firm I am employed with are most helpful and do consider disabled people'. Two young men referred to their work as 'better than being on the dole' and two to the opportunity it provided for them to use the training they had at St Loye's.

In a review of the literature on the transition to work Clarke (1978) reported that although many school leavers do not realize their aspirations, a large proportion express satisfaction with the jobs they obtain. Clarke adds the cautionary note that such satisfaction may be short-lived if it is the outcome of negative feelings about school, the novelty of working, having independence and earning money. This short-lived satisfaction may apply to some of the young people in this study, though many will have been working for some time. When asked whether or not they expected to be doing the same type of work in three years' time, 51 per cent replied that they didn't know. This may reflect their uncertainty about the prospect of redundancies or potential dissatisfaction with the actual work. One young clerk for example, felt that he was satisfied with his job and expected to be doing the same kind of work for some time but had added, 'More advanced though I hope'. Forty-three per cent of the respondents answered that they did expect to be in the same kind of work in three years' time and six per cent did not expect to be.

Aspirations

All the young people interviewed were asked about their 'dream' job, in the sense of a job that they would most like to do that was within their capabilities. What perhaps was most striking was the 'fit' between their aspirations and the type of work they were either look-ing for, or indeed, employed in. Just over half of the interviewees gave a reply that matched exactly their present or hoped-for employment. As one young man replied, 'Possibly the job I'm doing now, always been happy doing what I am doing at the moment.' A few inter-viewees were unable to answer this question and just remarked, 'Any-thing I could cope with' or 'Something safe for me to do'.

There were three young women who said that they would like to work with young children. One of them who was confined to a wheel-chair said that she felt she could do so if given the chance, but she knew that she wouldn't have a hope of being chosen for such work. People are, she suggested, wary of letting you look after children. Another woman who had mild left-sided hemiplegia felt that she got on with children all right and had worked with them as part of her school curriculum. She had then been told that she would not be able to find such work because of her disability. Two young men expressed keen interest in becoming car mechanics and had both studied the subject at school, which had, no doubt, fuelled their ambition. Indeed, one had obtained a CSE (Grade I) in Car Mechanics, only to be told that because of his weak legs he would never obtain such employment.

There were only three young people who expressed ambitions beyond those which could reasonably be attained by similar able-bodied young people. One would have liked to have been an interior designer if 'I had had more brains', another aspired to working for the BBC as a cameraman because he would have enjoyed the travel. There was only one interviewee, a young man who was a thalidomide victim, who was truly fired with enthusiasm, suggesting that he would like to spend more time Hot Rod racing and making a career out of what was a hobby. It was his dream because of the 'sheer danger, power, speed of cars, the crowds and the showing people it can be done'.

In his Sheffield study Carter (1962) found that only a third of the boys and a half of the girls entered the types of jobs for which they were aiming. A study in London, Maizels (1970), found that only a third of the school leavers questioned obtained jobs which were in line with their stated aspirations. These studies differ from the present one in that the information was gathered before the young people had had any experience of training or employment. At work individuals may look for and obtain the available satisfactions, i.e. there may be an adjustment to the reality of the work situation. It may also be, however, that for some people the satisfaction gained from their achievements in a subject at St Loye's was reflected in their realistic work aspirations and several people did express considerable pride in their training.

Disappointments

Younghusband (1970) suggested that there are two criteria by which successful adaptations to handicap are judged in adult life: the ability to earn a living and the ability to lead an independent life. Certainly it is difficult to exaggerate the psychological importance work has for most people. The Work Ethic carries considerable weight in contemporary society and implies that people should work irrespective of financial reward or type of work – that it is in some way morally good to work. The stigma and hardship of unemployment that reflect social values may lessen as unemployment in the general population rises, yet they may have considerable impact on those currently unemployed. As one young man in this study, who had been unemployed for nearly two years, suggested unemployment means a shortage of money, being partly dependent on parents, too much spare time and a 'feeling of being useless and unwanted'.

Respondents were asked what, if anything, they disliked about being unemployed. Not everyone completed this question but for those who did, the most frequently mentioned 'dislike' was boredom, with lack of money being next in order of importance. Forty-eight young people answered this question on the questionnaire, and they gave between them, 73 responses. Forty-seven per cent of these responses related to boredom, 27 per cent to lack of money, ten per cent to a feeling of being useless, ten per cent to social isolation and the remainder to other negative feelings such as frustration and depression.

This boredom and feeling of uselessness was expanded on by those young people interviewed. One young man when asked how he spent his time shrugged and announced sheepishly 'Oh, all right, I'll tell you then'. Apparently, his day typically consisted of getting up at noon and watching the television until it finished. He went out when he could afford it to the local pub to play dominoes, and the PHAB (Physically Handicapped and Able-Bodied) Club provided welcome relief every Tuesday evening. In the three years since leaving St Loye's he had completed two work-experience posts, both lasting for six months and had been unemployed ever since. To have come from four terms of further education and a three month training course at St Loye's to two years of unemployment where 'I don't go out in the afternoons, I just sit in the house. Don't bother to go to a cafe, rather sit in my armchair' indicates a considerable waste both of resources and human potential. Perhaps surprisingly he was still optimistic about finding employment claiming that 'Sometimes disabled people do get good jobs. I want to get to that level'. Another young man who had been unemployed in the 18 months since leaving St Loye's expressed his dissatisfaction with not working by saying, 'Having a lot of time to waste is sad. Trying to get myself out of bed in the morning and knowing there is nothing to do'.

There were two young men in this study who claimed not to be interested in finding a job because they didn't feel that it was worth it. One had been unemployed in the 3½ years since leaving the College and had made numerous attempts to find work. There was one book-keeping job (his training trade) that he would have liked but had his interview been successful he probably would have had to turn it down because the design of the building made access a problem. He had stopped seriously job-hunting about a year ago and described the period from Monday to Friday each week as a 'complete blank'. The enthusiasm and confidence acquired at College had gradually gone, he claimed, and his disillusionment is perhaps not surprising. The other young man had been unemployed for 4½ of the five years since leaving College, having managed to secure a six-month trial with one company after giving a talk at a meeting concerned with the employment of disabled people. He claimed that he was told that he would not be kept on two days before the end of the trial period and felt bitter at being given a taste of work only to be rejected. He felt that some people concerned with his education and training had stressed the likelihood of his obtaining employment and created in him an unrealistic attitude of 'thinking I'd walk straight into a job'. Rather than being a 'bed of roses' life after college was 'hard, very hard'. These two young men, having sought work for some considerable length of time, seemed resigned to an unemployed future.

Perhaps what is surprising is that only two young people felt that it was not worth looking for employment. As Greaves and Massie (op.cit.) point out, many disabled people are in low-paid jobs with little chance of promotion. They suggest that there may be little virtue in grappling both with a disability and a low income if one can live as well without work and its consequent anxiety. Yet, as the optimism and enthusiasm of one young woman show, most people do feel it is worthwhile. She wrote,'I get fed up being at home all the time, I can't wait to start work'. She had been unemployed for nearly three years since leaving St Loye's with presumably little prospect of finding suit-able employment. The strong desire to obtain employment was indicated by the number of young people who took exception to being asked 'What, if anything, do you like about being unemployed?'. One young woman wrote, 'Like, you must be joking!' and another emphasized in capital letters, 'THIS IS A STUPID QUESTION!'. The position of young unemployed people may worsen significantly as time goes by, as a good employment record may be an important factor in obtaining work and the motivation shown by having been to college may be dissipated by the effects of long periods of unemployment.

Striking a balance

It was concern with the fact that many disabled young people are unable to obtain and keep open employment that prompted Glanville (1974) to suggest that we should be looking at ways of enabling such people to make a real and practical contribution to society other than through success in employment. The point is well made. The issue is, however, extremely complex and considerable care must be exercised by those responsible for young people who feel themselves to be capable of employment. There is, as Glanville suggests, a danger of creating an ideal of open employment that many will not attain, and of leaving them without a safety-net of useful activity. The implications of designating young people unemployable are equally problematic. There are disabled people (see for example Bleackley (1974)) who have proved beyond doubt that the cliché 'disability does not mean inability' is most certainly true. Employers of disabled employees are in the majority of cases very positive about their employment as the review by Kettle (op.cit.) and this present study show. It is impossible to predict who will or will not obtain employment and attempts to do so would be retrogressive in view of the difficult and hard-won steps forward that disabled people have been able to make in terms of employment.

Disabled people often have to contend not only with their physical disability but with the reactions of other people and their misunderstanding (what could be termed prejudice). It therefore seems unjust that they should then be restricted by being denied access to further education and training, because they have been labelled 'unemployable'. In a recent study concerned with children with spina bifida (Hunt, 1981), it was suggested that only very few of the 100 children studied will enter normal employment and that many will require a period of education and training beyond the usual school leaving age. The latter part of that statement is certainly in line with the current thinking of those involved in the education of young people with special needs. Many disabled young people could benefit from post-school education as, of course, could and do many of their able-bodied peers. Hunt's suggestion that it would be unrealistic to

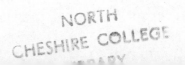

aim higher than a repetitive, sedentary job in a sheltered environment for the majority of these young people may be not only factually incorrect, but damaging to the efforts made to educate people about the abilities of disabled people.

What does seem to be essential is a realistic appraisal of the possibilities that may confront a young person and perhaps more emphasis on the 'safety net' discussed by Glanville (op.cit.) would be appropriate. Warnock (op.cit.) suggested that disabled people may find the 'secret of significant living without work' in voluntary social and community work. This may indeed fulfil a need for many disabled people, providing that they do not have to commit themselves in such a way as to jeopardize their supplementary benefit (if claimed). Certainly leisure as presently viewed cannot effectively replace the structure provided by work in an individual's life. Going to work involves an obligation and a need to meet expectations from significant others which few leisure activities can provide.

An education that aims to develop young people not only academically and vocationally, but also socially and personally may better equip them for the future. As a recent report by the Further Education Curriculum Review and Development Unit (FEU, 1980) suggests there is a growing recognition of the importance of personal and social factors in the workplace. The concept of transferability was discussed in another FEU publication (1979) and defined as 'the learning of generally applicable skills and capacities and the ability to transfer them – even if the vehicle for learning is an interest in *one* vocational sector'. This report suggests that a post-16 pre-employment course should consist of:

> core studies – those studies to which all students of this age should have right of access, and that learning which is common to all vocational preparation including induction;
>
> vocational studies – that learning which is particular to a given vocational sector. (E.g. hotel and catering, repair and maintenance);
>
> job-specific studies – that learning which is particular to a given job within a sector.

Such changes in curricula are innovatory and may provoke opposition from those who prefer vocational training to concentrate more narrowly than the suggestions above. The FEU report (1979) suggests that care should be taken that the traditional courses do not dominate the curriculum of vocational studies at the expense of 'an up-to-date and realistic analysis of demands which are made on young people, now entering that sector'. Both FEU reports cited above are concerned with ordinary education and indicate the direction currently being taken by those involved in curriculum design. The principles underlying this thinking are no less relevant in special further education.

The main points raised by this chapter are summarized below.

- The vast majority of young people currently in employment felt that they were satisfied with their work and the most frequently given reason why related to the content of the work. The caution was added that this satisfaction may be relatively short-lived, particularly for those young people with limited opportunities for promotion. Half of the respondents did not know whether or not they would be doing the same kind of work in three years' time.

- There was considerable 'fit' between the work aspirations of the young people interviewed and their present or hoped-for employment. The importance of the satisfaction they had gained from the education and training at St Loye's was mentioned.

- The unemployed young people provided evidence of the boredom, financial difficulty and feeling of uselessness that unemployment can bring.

- The dilemma of finding a balance between discouraging young people in terms of employment and presenting them with an unrealistic goal was discussed. It was suggested that a broadened revised curriculum may be advantageous.

CHAPTER FOUR

Job Placement

The previous chapters discussed the employment histories of the young people in this study and the situation of those who are unemployed. This chapter is concerned with how young people find employment and their perceptions of the facilities available to them. Who is there to provide a service to young people when they leave St Loye's? How do they hear about their jobs? Who helps them in their job search and whose help do they find most useful?

The Personnel

The specialist careers officer (SCO) is, for most of these young people, a person they had contact with during their schooldays who suggested and organized their application to St Loye's. This person will have had a termly report on each student in his or her authority and may have been consulted about employment prospects in the area for particular young people. The SCO therefore is ideally placed to be involved in the move from St Loye's. It is, however, fortunate for young people leaving St Loye's that the SCO is, in many cases, able to 'join forces' with another worker, the Manpower Services Commission's disablement resettlement officer (DRO). The Careers Service is available to young people until they are 19 or 20 and the MSC is able to offer help to those aged over 16. The relatively detailed knowledge which the SCO has of the young person and his or her background may be usefully combined with the greater range of services available from the DRO. Such services include registration, assistance with fares to work, aids and adaptations and job introduction schemes. Both the SCO and DRO will have experience and knowledge of the employers in their area and of job opportunities.

Greaves and Massie (op.cit.) found after interviewing a number of DROs and Senior DROs that while 'one would hope that the co-operation between the SCO and DROs would be close . . . we have found in many cases this is not so'. More co-operation between these two agencies could clarify what is after all a complex and confusing area. This confusion was experienced by one of the young people interviewed – he had gone to see his DRO after leaving St Loye's and had been directed back to his SCO as he was at that time 18. Exclusion from the help of the DRO had heightened his conviction that the Disablement Resettlement Service was of more use to him than the Careers Service and he was frustrated by being unable to register as a disabled person – 'I thought I could have a disabled card (Green Card given on registration) what with being to a disabled college'. This young man's feeling of being denied a service 'that is after all for the disabled' was reflected in a rather negative attitude towards his careers officer, an attitude no doubt reinforced by the fact that he found his present job through a friend who used to work at the firm on Saturdays. Another respondent suggested that 'Nobody seemed really interested and they couldn't seem to make up their minds if I came under the Jobcentre or Careers Office!'

One service of the DRO already mentioned is registration. Any person who is capable of, and looking for, work but who is disabled in such a way as to need special help with placing, can register with the Disabled Persons Register. There are benefits to be gained from registration such as eligibility for sheltered employment, designated employment, the quota system and fares to work assistance. The last service may prove useful, as may access to sheltered work, but the role of the quota system and designated employment are less obvious. The quota system is a means by which any employer who employs more than 20 people is obliged to employ a quota of registered disabled people – three per cent of the total. In practice this obligation is not strictly enforced and a large number of employers do not have their quota of disabled people. The Manpower Services Commission has recently suggested that the quota system be abolished in favour of new legislation placing a general statutory duty on employers to take reasonable steps to promote equality of opportunity for disabled people. As regards designated employment there are two jobs to be held exclusively by registered disabled people (unless none are available), namely car-park attendant and lift attendant. Such designations are hardly a major step forward in relation to the employment of disabled people, particularly in view of the increasing mechanization of car-parks and the prevalence of escalators and unmanned lifts.

One DRO interviewed during this research felt that the benefits to be gained from registration were in many cases not enough to outweigh the possible 'labelling' effect and suggested that he often had to remind himself at least to offer new clients the opportunity to register. Indeed, the number of disabled people registering has steadily decreased from 494,877 in April 1979, to 482,006 in 1980 and 470,588 in 1981. Nevertheless, 75 per cent of the young people in this study were registered as disabled, 14 per cent were not and nine per cent didn't know either way. (Two per cent of respondents did not complete this question.) Most of the people who did not know whether or not they were registered had had contact with their DRO, which suggests a need for more clarification of the system for some clients. A few had gone straight into work found through the careers officer, St Loye's staff or family contacts. Rather less than half of those who said that they were not registered as disabled had had contact with their DRO which may be indicative of an informed choice having been made. Such a choice may create difficulties as in the case of one young woman who found that the 'Careers Officer was rude and discouraging due to my unwillingness to register as a disabled person'. It may be easy in a world that lumps 'the disabled' together to lose sight of the fact that the classifications devised by administrators may not always tally with the individual aspirations of those so classified. Those people who had not registered and had not seen their DRO had in the main, found employment without recourse to official agencies. In such cases the benefits available from the DRO may be unknown to them and their employers. If the DROs are to be seen as providing more than just a placement service then it is important that facilities available from them are utilized to the full. As one DRO suggested, 'I should be out there every afternoon with employers, but I just don't have the time.' Ideally, the DROs' work would include a percentage of time for educating the public.

Sources of information

Respondents to the questionnaire were asked how they heard about their jobs. Looking at all jobs obtained (i.e. could be up to six for any one individual), the Jobcentre was the most frequently mentioned source of information, accounting for 28 per cent of all jobs. Answers were coded 'Jobcentre' only when the respondent actually used those words, but the phrase may have been used, in general terms, when in fact a DRO had been seen. However, those respondents who were interviewed did seem to make a clear distinction between using the Jobcentre and seeing personnel and seemed to make regular use of the former. When asked about seeking employment a typical response from an interviewee was, 'Well, I have a look in the Jobcentre most days'. Twenty-one per cent of all jobs obtained followed information from friends or family, 15 per cent from DROs, 12 per cent from media sources (mainly the evening paper) and 11 per cent from SCOs. The remaining 13 per cent of jobs found came from information such as that obtained from St Loye's College or from social workers or from the employee's own initiative. One young man replied to the question, 'I just went along and asked the manager if he had any jobs going'. These figures contrast with those given by Walker (1980) who found that 39 per cent of jobs were gained through informal sources (family and friends) and 19 per cent through the Careers Service.

Respondents were asked to provide separate information for each of their jobs and this again indicates the consistent use made of the Jobcentre. Twenty-two per cent of all first jobs followed information from the Jobcentre as did 37 per cent and 46 per cent of second and third jobs respectively. Information from DROs and family or friends both accounted for the same number of first job placements – 19 per cent. Media sources were not used extensively for the first placements, accounting for only eight per cent, with SCOs giving information for 14 per cent and miscellaneous sources, already referred to, accounting for the rest.

As regards second job placements, the second most useful source of information (following the Jobcentre) was family or friends which accounted for 21 per cent of jobs found. The media increased in importance providing information on 16 per cent of all placements with the DRO and SCO accounting for 12 per cent and seven per cent of all information on jobs respectively. Again the remaining seven per cent heard about their jobs from miscellaneous sources. Of the 13 people who had obtained a third job, the media had provided information for three of them (the second most important source after the Jobcentre), family and friends two, and the SCO one. The number of young people involved in fourth, fifth or sixth placements was extremely small though their sources of information followed the same trend, in that the Jobcentre, the media and family or friends were involved. Informal sources of information about jobs did play an important part in job-finding for these young people which suggests the importance of equipping such people with necessary interview and application completion skills in order to maximize their independent approach. The figures for the sources of information about jobs are given in Table 4.1.

Table 4.1: Sources of information about jobs (n=185)

Source of information	% of jobs						Total % of jobs
	First n=116	Second n=43	Third n=13	Fourth n=7	Fifth n=5	Sixth n=1	
Disablement Resettlement Officer	19	12	–	–	–	–	15
Specialist Careers Officer	14	7	8	–	–	–	11
Jobcentre	22	37	46	14	20	–	28
Media	8	16	23	29	20	–	12
Family and friends	19	21	15	57	20	–	21
Other	18	7	8	–	40	100	13

For those people who had obtained sheltered employment, as might be expected, the DRO was most important in providing information about the work. Indeed all but two of the young people so employed had used this service and one of them had heard from a friend, while the other had been informed by his social worker. The Youth Opportunities Programmes had usually been heard about from the SCO.

The figures above relating to sources of information are important in that they quantify sources that resulted in specific job placements. They do not however indicate whether such placements were long-term or whether they were satisfactory. The numbers involved in this study are small, but they show that 50 per cent of the young people placed through the DRO or SCO are still in that first placement, as are 43 per cent of those placed through family or friends. Only 35 per cent of those who obtained a first placement from a Jobcentre are still in that job which perhaps indicates that some young people had selected inappropriate work and had insufficient guidance. Four of the young people had used the Jobcentre repeatedly and were currently unemployed. The decreasing role played by the professional services in placements after the initial one may indicate a reluctance by young people to return to them or an inability by hard-pressed services to respond to young people who have already been placed. There were only two young people, for example, who had been placed twice by the DRO and they had both been made redundant from the initial placement.

Hów the contact was perceived

Information about the contact that the young people had had with both official and informal sources of help with employment was sought and respondents were asked whether or not this contact had been useful. The data about contacts made in relation to job-hunting suffer because when people had not answered a particular question it was not known whether they had actually not had contact or had just omitted to answer the question. The inclusion of a 'no contact' option on the question attempted to clarify this point but was not always used by respondents. Figures are given therefore for the number of people who reported contact rather than the percentages who did so.

Of the 108 people who reported having had contact with their DRO 59 per cent felt that it had been useful and although rather fewer of the young people reported contact with their SCO (88 did), a similar proportion – 53 per cent – found the contact useful. It may be that the guidance and support role of these services was extremely important. The definition of useful contact was left to the respondent and, clearly, many of them felt that their usefulness went beyond successful placement in a particular job. Roberts (1977) reported that 'there is no study of school-leavers in Britain in which the Careers Service, Careers Teachers, or any other body offering vocational guidance has emerged as a major influence'. As Roberts points out such research findings are misplaced if used as criticisms of the service. Much of the work of DROs and SCOs is, by its very nature 'back-room' work. One DRO told of how she had toured businesses in the area, knowing that a young woman in a wheelchair was soon to leave St Loye's. The Monday after leaving college this young woman had gone to her

DRO, the phone had rung and somebody had wanted a telephonist. Was the building suitable for a wheelchair-bound person? Yes. When could she come over? Straight away. No wonder the DRO shrugged! One SCO said, 'How can I tell them how many contacts or visits I have to make before somebody will have a look at them. It's so soul-destroying.' Of the 63 people who reported contact with friends about job-finding nearly 60 per cent found such contact useful and 56 per cent of the 34 people who had had such contact with the staff at St Loye's found it useful.

General satisfaction with a service or system of support may be difficult to quantify and it may be useful to examine the reasons given for dissatisfaction. Fifty-six per cent of respondents stated that they were satisfied with the help they had received in looking for work. The 50 people (33 per cent) who were not satisfied with the help were all able to give a reason. (Eleven per cent of respondents did not answer this question.) Hill *et al.* (1973) found evidence to suggest that a substantial minority of their respondents felt some sense of dissatisfaction with the employment services available to them and obviously people who are experiencing the stress and disappointment of unemployment may direct their attack at front line services. In the present study however, 42 per cent of those who said they were dissatisfied were currently in paid employment of some kind. One young man complained that he had faced a lack of understanding about the handicap of being deaf. He stated that he had had useful contact with his DRO, as had several other people in this 'dissatisfied' group.

One young man, currently on a work experience scheme, wrote 'without proper back-up from DROs it is almost a complete waste of time sending young people like myself to St Loye's because of our inexperience prior to training'. Given a national college that is training for specific jobs the liaison between the placement services in the home area and the staff at St Loye's is crucial if the assumption is made that the young person will go back to his or her home area. Obviously, the pressures on the SCO's and DRO's time will have implications for the clients' perception of them. One young man, also on work experience, wrote that he '. . . expected a little more help from our DRO officer, what can be gained by a 5-minute meeting, he has given me three meetings, it was a waste of time'. Another young man who had found his job through the paper wrote '. . . I had no indication which firms were more likely to take disabled people or how to go about it. DRO wasn't much help'. Other people spoke of feeling that staff were not interested or encouraging or as one young woman expressed it 'didn't give a hoot'. However, very few of the young people interviewed were wholly negative and several spoke warmly of both the personalities of those they had received professional help from and the help given. Small kindnesses were remembered – one DRO had offered to make a photocopy of one young man's St Loye's diploma so that he could send it to his prospective employer.

It was not the case that the young people in this study had ill-informed or unrealistic ideas about what work they were capable of, but it may be difficult for those giving guidance and support to give the right amount of encouragement. This point is made by Reynolds (1980) who found that 'In the present climate, particularly, a visit to the careers officer can be the first in a long series of discouragements that act as a mental impediment to young people trying to get out into the world' and then continued 'A worse picture emerged when it came to the DROs . . .'. One young man in this study who had obtained a post as assistant to the Managing Director through his local paper, a post that he liked as it provided variety, responsibility and the demand for accurate calculations, complained that he had not been encouraged to look for 'the kind of job you would want to do yourself'.

One young woman explained that she had, after discussion with her parents, decided not to take up employment that had been arranged by her SCO. She had spina bifida and was confined to a wheelchair and felt that having to cross a railway line every day to get to work (which would mean asking passers-by for help) and running the risk of getting chilblains in winter in a small detached office out-weighed the positive gains of having employment, especially as 'it was only temporary anyway'. Her SCO, on the other hand, claimed to have 'washed her hands' of the young woman as she had turned down, in the SCO's mind, a perfectly good job. The situation is fraught. Given that many placements of disabled people will involve consider-able time, effort and energy a situation may well arise in which any job is regarded as a good job. The point was made by Greaves and Massie (op.cit.) that there is a tendency 'only too widespread to consider that a disabled worker should be grateful for a job regardless of financial reward, the type of work or promotion prospects'.

In an article concerned with handicapped school-leavers, Walker and Lewis (1977) found among the young people interviewed 'a variety of perceptions of the role of the Careers Service'. They suggested that young people, failing to recognize the support given by the careers officer, may come to regard him as 'useless'. This clearly may occur where the aims and goals of the Careers Service are perceived differently by the officer and the young client. Roberts (op.cit.) suggests that in a situation where people typically don't choose jobs, but rather take what is available the careers officer should deal only with the practical employment problems rather than guidance. The point is reiterated by Walker and Lewis (op.cit.) who suggest that the placement function of the Careers Service is, rightly or wrongly, the basis on which it is judged by its clients. On the other hand there were young people in this study who found contact with official sources useful even when it did not lead to an actual job placement and one interviewee's comments suggest why. 'You need someone to be vying for you. Especially for a disabled person, need careers officers as employers take people like me at face value, need support from careers officers or anybody else, they can push out, they get listened to, it's moral support anyway.' In a largely able-bodied society, where disability is often equated with inability, such moral support may be essential.

The work of DROs and SCOs is often depressing and difficult. They may feel disheartened by placement figures, knowing that the MSC's success rate in placing disabled persons in jobs fell by 21.5 per cent and 36 per cent respectively in the second and third quarters of 1980 compared to the same period in the previous year. Looking at the overall placings of disabled people, the figure for 1979/80 was 59,736 and for 1980/81 it had fallen considerably to 39,466. The people in such work have usually had experience in the mainstream part of the service and as one SCO suggested 'You'd really have to want to do this work to do it'. It is a specialist job, that may be undertaken after (or indeed before) an extremely short training period for what is a complex and far-reaching subject area. Although specialist training received by DROs is considerably longer than that for SCOs it still amounts to a matter of weeks, and however intensive such training is there must, given the breadth of the specialism, be many gaps. One DRO felt that the training he had received had been good, given the time available, but felt that he could certainly profit from in-service sessions particularly as he felt ill-equipped to deal with people who had come from psychiatric hospitals and those with communication difficulties.

SCOs and DROs cannot make jobs better or create them. Unemployment has deep psychological effects and a client may be at his or her most unlikeable and least promising when depressed, self-pitying, resentful or demanding. One young man interviewed had written several letters to his MP, the MSC and Jack Ashley, MP, complaining of the ineffectiveness of the services available. He was assertive and disillusioned and seemed to have tried the patience of the DRO who had, he claimed, told him in an outburst of temper that he was well off (he had suffered extensive and severe burns to his neck and upper part of his body) and that people were much more badly wounded during the war. This young man's frustrations may seem threatening to those in receipt of them but perhaps such activism is preferable to the helplessness and resignation felt by many unemployed people.

There is clearly an element of 'marketing' in the placement of disabled people, given the misinformed and misguided views held by many able-bodied people about them. The problems this creates for those who have epilepsy is mentioned in this report and considerable effort may be expended in educating and explaining to employers. Lord Gowrie, the Minister of Employment, in a recent interview (22.3.81) stated that he felt legislative measures (the much-abused quota system) were not the way forward and stressed the role of education in changing the situation of disabled people. National campaigns are undertaken, but those may have little effect without back-up from personnel. As one DRO suggested 'Employers are fed up with all this mass of material they keep getting sent. The "good" employers aren't interested in getting awards anyway'. (A reference to the 'Fit for Work' award available to the employers of disabled people from the MSC.)

Those people currently unemployed

People who were unemployed were asked why they thought they hadn't got a job and a large minority, 47 per cent, of those who answered gave a reason that related to their physical disability. There were only five people, however, who gave as the reason their medical condition. One young man suffered from Friedreich's ataxia, a disease that had become significantly worse since he had left St Loye's, and another was recovering from major heart surgery.

There were two people who felt that suitable access to premises was the main factor. One young man had obtained work as an audit clerk through his DRO and had had to leave after a few months due to 'unsuitable premises'. Asked about any difficulties at work he had written 'Steps!' The remaining 'disability related' answers (by far the majority) suggested that the real disadvantage of disability had to do with other people's responses rather than with the disabling condition itself. One young woman wrote 'Because employers won't employ disabled people if they can avoid it'. Obviously, feelings of inadequacy or failure may be focussed on one's physical disability and other issues may be obscured. However, the comments made that do indicate the importance of societal responses to disability surely indicate a need for more 'marketing' of disabled workers and highlight the importance of collecting evidence from the employers of disabled people (see Chapter Two). The case was most strikingly made by three young people who suffered from epilepsy. They reported

'Employers seem to lose interest when my disability (well-controlled epilepsy) is mentioned at interviews';

'Most employers either don't understand epilepsy or they are frightened or think that people with epilepsy are nutters or something of that nature';

'People think just 'cos you've got it, you wriggle on the ground like a half-drowned rat, when you have an attack.'

The second most common reason given for being unemployed was the general climate of high unemployment and the third was what could be termed a personal orientation. In the former grouping a typical comment was 'I think I haven't got a job because of the unemployment situation and the shortage of jobs'. One young woman felt that her unemployment was 'due to the recession in Industry'.

Clearly redundancy has played a role in the employment history of young people in the study (this was detailed in Chapter Two). The fact remains however that unemployment among disabled people is higher than among able-bodied people. In March 1980 12.6 per cent of registered disabled people were unemployed compared with six per cent of the general population. Figures available in March 1981 indicate that the unemployment rate for registered disabled people (15.3 per cent) is rising more slowly than the rate for the rest of the population (10.1 per cent). One worrying aspect of the idea that the recession has taken over is that people may then lose enthusiasm and hope as regards job-hunting. As one DRO suggested 'I do need to impress upon people that there are jobs to be had and they can still try. I don't let them get away with saying they needn't look because of the cuts'.

The reasons given for present unemployment that had a personal orientation were divided equally into two groups. One was based on personal characteristics and one on external factors pertinent to the individual. One young man in the first group who was confined to a wheelchair felt that his 'lack of confidence in myself, not enough attempts at getting one (a job) and the usual reasons, no access etc' were major factors. Another respondent blamed herself. She was currently attending a day centre and felt that she was unemployed 'because I could not settle down at St Loye's long enough to learn a job'. In the second group a young woman who trained as a typist/telephonist at St Loye's and in the three years and four months since leaving had only worked on a nine-month work experience scheme wrote that, 'They couldn't keep me on. I'm just unlucky and haven't had the opportunity. They either want you to have experience or you have too much to do that you wouldn't be able to cope.' The other external factor mentioned was lack of training.

Respondents who were unemployed and seeking employment were asked how they went about looking for suitable work. The vast majority (78 per cent) of people who answered this question gave at least two sources used to find employment. From the people interviewed it was clear that most people living in towns are able to visit the Jobcentre regularly, but for those in rural areas, even assuming that they could use public transport, the cost involved was prohibitive. There were three people currently unemployed but seeking employment who had used the services of a private employment agency. There was no evidence in this study to corroborate Greaves and Massie's (op.cit.) suggestion that many disabled people thought that it was the DROs function to find them a job while in the meantime they could sit at home and wait. One young man had replied to over 60 job advertisements and visited the Jobcentre regularly. Another who said that he had been to his Jobcentre regularly where his DRO has been trying very hard to find him employment had had 46 interviews for work. A third who had only worked for three weeks in the 31 months since leaving St Loye's had been employed as a labourer but was made redundant when the site closed down. His disillusionment was clear. He stated that he didn't do a lot now about finding a job, but that when he'd come out of St Loye's he was trying for one 'practically every day'. His tone of acceptance and belief that 'the chance of me getting a job is around 100 to 1' are disturbing. The main points raised in this chapter are discussed below.

- Information collected about how people heard about jobs they had obtained showed the use made of the Jobcentre and family and friends.

- The usefulness of the professional placing services even when they did not provide information about jobs obtained was indicated by the young people in this study.

- A third of the young people, many of whom are in employment, expressed some dissatisfaction with the help available to them. Several comments related to lack of encouragement or time given by staff in the placement services.

- The importance of public education about disabled people was discussed and it was said that the professional placement services have an important role to play.

- The considerable efforts made by those young people currently employed to obtain work were discussed.

CHAPTER FIVE

Personal Development

This chapter does not attempt to provide a typical picture of the lives of young disabled people. Rather it is hoped that the individual experiences described here illustrate both the variety of situations in which disabled people find themselves and the variety of responses or coping mechanisms available to them. Adolescence has been described by Rutter (1980) as 'the link between immaturity and maturity' when young people 'carry the strengths and scars established in childhood and look forward to the adult world – but are not quite part of either'. Dorner (1977) has suggested that 'Adolescence is known to be a time of problems with crucial issues of independence, work, training, relationships with the opposite sex and so on'. There has however been little study of the particular situation of disabled adolescents. Rowan (op.cit.) suggested that 'the adolescent was chosen for study both because of the lack of research and development work at this age level and because the stage between childhood and the adult world represents a particularly critical turning point for the handicapped'. The young people in this study had spent a proportion of their adolescent years at St Loye's College and presumably had had to cope not only with the problems Dorner describes, but also with their physical disability and the reactions of other people to that disability.

'Sometimes I feel like wearing a sandwich board saying that I may be in a wheelchair but that I'm not stupid!'

Classifying people into groups and establishing internal predictors as to where they will be encountered and how they will behave, enable the members of the society to organize and simplify their interactions with others. The concept of stigma which is explored by Goffman (1963) may be a by-product of this process of classification. He writes that 'While the stranger is present before us, evidence can arise of his possessing an attribute that makes him different from others in the category of persons available for him to be, and of a less desirable kind – in the extreme, a person who is quite thoroughly bad, or dangerous, or weak. He is thus reduced in our minds from a whole and usual person to a tainted, discounted one'. A physical disability is an example of the attributes that Goffman described as 'deeply discrediting' and an individual with such a stigma may find that he or she is unsure of how able-bodied people will identify and receive him or her. One young woman in this study who has cerebral palsy and is confined to a wheelchair spoke of the distress she felt when people she encountered spoke down to her and treated her as if she was 'stupid in the head'. Her experience of the 'Does he take sugar?' syndrome caused her considerable anguish as she felt, for example, that when she went to the local pub with her sister and mother, even local people who had known her and her family for several years would be too embarrassed to speak to her, though they would chat about her to her family. As she suggested 'People who know me don't think of the wheelchair' and her sense of alienation was expressed in her comment that 'I am Jane, not a poor little girl sitting in a wheelchair'.

A paper from the Central Council for Education and Training in Social Work (1974) described the tendency (of people in a largely able-bodied society) to regard a handicapped person as being a different kind of person, to assume that he or she doesn't have the same human needs, desires and aspirations as non-disabled people. The report spoke of the dislike that disabled people had of the stereotyped view that most able-bodied people take and of their concern that a handicap is frequently regarded as their most significant if not their only notable attribute. As Carver and Rodda (1978) suggest being disabled is often interpreted as belonging to a different and probably inferior order of beings. A recent study by Weir (op.cit.) showed the confusion many members of the general public feel about people who are handicapped. People who are misinformed may so easily group together people who are physically and mentally handicapped or may assume that all physically disabled people are 'ill' and needing constant hospital attendance which will disrupt their work

and education. The very words *handicap* and *disability* seem to con-
jure up certain extremely restricted images for those who are uninformed. There are disabled people who achieve success in remarkable
and obvious ways – the man who takes part in outdoor pursuits
despite having no legs and the girl whose sense of humour and personality are said to overcome her physical disability. Such achievements
are not to be discounted and clearly they indicate to those who think
otherwise that disabled people do have characteristics and abilities
that go far beyond their apparent disability. An emphasis on the
'characters' among disabled people is however still removed from the
stage where disabled people are viewed as individuals and can behave
as such without causing embarrassment or confusion. Indeed the
exclusion of outstanding personalities or first-hand experience from
the stereotype may serve to maintain that stereotype.

The invasions of privacy that disabled people may encounter is
commented on by Goffman (op.cit.) when he speaks of 'the conversations strangers may feel free to strike up with him, conversations in
which they express what he takes to be morbid curiosity about his
condition, or in which they proffer help that he does not need or want'.
Goffman refers to the 'classic formulae' for these kinds of conversations and speaks of the implication behind them that 'the stigmatised
individual is a person who can be approached by strangers at will,
providing only that they are sympathetic to the plight of persons of his
kind'. The young woman already mentioned reported how people
often came up to her and inquired 'Are you all right dear?' She
recalled how a colleague had suggested that they all walk over to the
pub and had been extremely apologetic and distressed when she
realised the inappropriateness of the word. However, for Jane this had
been 'the best compliment I've ever had' because her colleague had
shown that 'she didn't think of me as a disabled person'. A young man
who has spina bifida and normally uses a wheelchair spoke warmly of
his sister's boyfriend who is 'the only person I can call a friend' and
who, much to his delight, 'treats me as a normal person'. The ques-
tionable use of the word 'normal' was commented on by one rather
self-possessed young woman at the end of her interview when she said
'What's normal anyway? We all have defects, it's just that ours show
up'.

The social interaction between disabled and able-bodied people
may, given the uneasiness sometimes felt by the participants, result in
the disabled person reacting with a defensive withdrawal or a seem-

ingly hostile bravado. Much of the difficulty may be due to an embarrassment on the part of the able-bodied person and an uncertainty about how to act in this unfamiliar situation. A disabled person needs to be able to cope with social interactions and sometimes with unpleasantness. One young woman who was confined to a wheelchair spoke of how she had been shopping in a large chain store one Saturday and had been accosted by a harrassed fellow-shopper, who had told her that 'people like her' shouldn't be allowed out into the shops on Saturday. The young woman had immediately replied that she worked during the week and that Saturday was the only chance she had to do her shopping. She was pleased that, at 21, she now had the presence of mind to do this and felt that 'a couple of years ago I'd have burst into tears!'

The information collected in this study on the employment histories of these young people provided evidence of the particular demands made on disabled people. One young woman, confined to a wheelchair, greatly valued the degree of independence she had achieved, and moved easily around her parents' home. She had gone for an interview and felt that so much of what the interviewer had had to say had started off with 'Of course you wouldn't be able to manage this'. The interviewer's down-grading of this applicant's ability, particularly regarding her agility with doors and mobility may have resulted from a genuine desire to be helpful. However, for this quietly spoken young woman the interview had been extremely threatening, and she had withdrawn, being unable to assert herself sufficiently. She had not been offered the job. Oswin (1978) described how a woman who was a qualified book-keeper and who had several certificates in commercial studies was asked by her interviewer at a job interview 'Can you write and add up'? Oswin suggests 'the interviewer was apparently so thrown at the sight of her disability and the fact that she was in a wheelchair that he did not know how to behave naturally'.

How do you spend your time?

'I'm going to sound incredibly dull. I get a meal, am busy cooking, clearing up, domestic things, washing, it's too expensive to go out at the present time – I read and watch TV.'

'I get bored very easily, there is the housework, I don't let the place get in a mess, do things in the morning, lost for things to do in the afternoon, I watch TV and make my rug.'

'Usually doing the housework during the day. Have joined the Young Farmers' Club, go off to dances now and again, hope to go to Bristol and go to things – a friend has just passed her driving test. Collect stamps, key-rings, do touch tapestry, anything that is going really, getting the tea.'

These three quotes are fairly typical of the comments made by interviewees when asked about their use of time. There were a few young people with fairly full social lives – one young man had several friends in the gang of 'lads' in his village that he had grown up with who provided company for his leisure time. Another young man belonged to three clubs that meet regularly, was positive about his attendance and was satisfied with his social life, apart from his 'desperate' need to find a girlfriend. These cases were, however, atypical and the comments received from interviewees substantiated those of Rowe and Morgan (1976) who found that most of the handicapped people in their study 'live very restricted social lives'. Dorner (op.cit.) found that for the young people with spina bifida in his study 'social isolation, not surprisingly is a very common problem'. As Dorner suggests 'This is sad because given the opportunity as at school, most teenagers appear well able to get on with their peers'. It is suggested in Chapter Six that attendance at a residential specialist college provides disabled young people with an opportunity to enjoy and benefit from a sense of peer group identity. The fact that so many young people felt happy with and enjoyed this opportunity makes their current position all the more striking.

Most of the young people interviewed did not have friends living locally and many had no one they would call a close friend, i.e. someone they particularly enjoyed seeing or could confide in. One young man spoke of the boredom of his present life of unemployment suggesting that you can build up friends at work but that 'It's difficult to do this in the dole queue'. While opportunities for social interaction do exist at work, it is worth noting that none of the young people in employment had friendships with colleagues that went beyond the working day, although they may have participated in group out-of-hours social mixing when, for example, a whole department would go out for a drink. The mother of one of the young hearing impaired young women interviewed spoke of how lonely her daughter had been, when she came home from St Loye's. She felt that everything was provided for them socially at St Loye's and that it was 'almost too easy for them' in that 'when they came home they didn't know what to do, didn't know anybody'. She added 'One thing you can't do for your children is get them friends'.

Membership of clubs and organizations was limited with only a few young people taking part in such activity. A few had been to PHAB clubs and two young men were very enthusiastic about the experience. One young woman who had been disappointed recalled her one and only visit to her local club and complained of the wide age-range of those attending. People had apparently worn name-tags and sat round having tea and biscuits. To her mind it was a 'glorified Darby and Joan club' and not at all what 21-year-olds do. She had stayed there for a while and then 'gone down the pub with my mum'. Several of the young people interviewed didn't want to go to such clubs as they felt that they didn't want to mix with other disabied people. One young woman had been to some sessions held locally for people with epilepsy but had not enjoyed them as the emphasis had been on the epilepsy and not the people who have it. She preferred to go out, as a couple with her husband, with friends who would treat her just as a person who happened to have epilepsy. Interviewees usually referred to able-bodied people as 'normal' and commented on people they knew or members of their family who treated them as though they were 'normal' as well.

The young people interviewed were asked about any evening classes they attended. One young woman was taking an accountancy course at her local technical college and described her social life as 'mostly staying at home and studying'. She is prepared to undertake this two-year course as she 'wanted to do a course that would give me promotion'. Another is attending adult literacy and numeracy classes and one young man is taking 'O' level maths at his local college of further education. One young woman had done a typing course for two evenings a week and would have liked to have attended the college full-time. She felt however that 'humping her wheelchair up and down the stairs' had been tolerable twice a week but made her full-time attendance impracticable.

Many people were dissatisfied with their social life and there would seem to be a need for more provision for leisure and for existing provision to be accessible. Many disabled people are likely to have a considerable amount of time on their hands and they could usefully learn how to use it. Two young people in wheelchairs spoke of being barred from their local cinema, even though both they and their escorts were sure that they could have made a swift exit if the need arose. This barring occurs so frequently in one town that the local Spastics Society are taking up the issue. Oswin (op.cit.) wrote of the 'Extraordinary regulations and lack of community understanding (that) often make it seem as if society deliberately aims to stigmatise handicapped people, and exclude them from ordinary enjoyments.'

'Everything's been done for you and then at 18 they send you back to your family and say "get on with it".'

Another related aspect of a disabled young person's development is that of independence. The staff on the residential side of the Further Education Unit are aware of a need to think ahead and realize that the residence is in some ways a sheltered, cosy environment. Residents are responsible for their own laundry and while all meals are taken in the dining room a training kitchen is available. It is hoped to expand the opportunities for the use of this kitchen as part of the aim of developing independence. The majority of the young people interviewed were living with their parents though many said they were dissatisfied with this. Some of this was expressed in terms of wanting more freedom and independence now and some in concern for the future. There were a few young people living at home with other siblings who felt that family relations were good and who enjoyed the present situation. As other members of the family leave home the position of those remaining will change and some expressed awareness of and concern about this fact.

> Alan was severely disabled, needed some help with his personal care and felt that he would love to leave home and have a place of his own and that the pressures of being at home all day surrounded by siblings (he is the eldest of six children) were oppressive. He worries considerably about what will happen to him 'when this lot (his siblings) go'. He gets depressed two or three times a week and feels that his home situation exacerbates this. Being at home means the same environment 'all day long day after day, same faces bound to get you down, that's why I'd rather be on my own. Everybody's on top of each other. I get very nasty if things don't go right, I have no patience, I go up in the air'.

This young man had attended a residential special school before St Loye's and was bitter about his position now. He felt that 'you have a sheltered environment all your life and then they kick you out and expect you to cope'. One young woman, who was married and shared an adapted maisonette with her husband, felt that young people at St Loye's should be given more idea of what the 'real world' is like and suggested that the College rent three or four flats and let people have a taste of independence, with the support of college staff. One young man had been very lonely and isolated for much of the two and a half years since leaving college but had now started to make friends through his interest in Citizen Band radios. He felt himself fortunate to have his own home and commented on the situation of those who were not so fortunate. 'They don't get on with their parents and have no social life when they go home. They go to St Loye's for a break, get away and then go back and might as well not have gone away as they can't use what they've done at college, they get to know people and then are chucked back into old surroundings. Should be somewhere they can go out and make a new start.' Oswin (op.cit.) wrote of 'the indignity of long-term hospital care, the mass routines and lack of home comforts' – a situation in which many of these young people may ultimately find themselves unless they are able to achieve a relatively independent life.

Certainly the young people interviewed provided evidence of housing needs, both in the immediate and long-term future. The Fokus housing scheme in Sweden provides evidence of how people with special needs can be successfully accommodated. Since 1964 Fokus has built more than 300 flats for disabled people placed in normal housing blocks all over the country. Staff are available at any time the residents want help, with supplementary staff paid to come in at the 'peak' morning, evening and lunchtime hours. The scheme at Fokus indicates the need for independence within limits, in the sense that for someone who takes an hour to dress him or her self the help of an able-bodied person at the appropriate time may suit him or her better than independence at whatever cost. Again, it is important to stress that many disabled people would not necessarily need the aids and adaptations so often thought of as a first priority. Someone who has epileptic fits, for example, may need nothing more than the reassurance that somebody will be available should he or she need assistance.

Fokus claim that over a third of the tenants are either married or living together and that before the provision was available to them less than ten per cent were. Only four of the young people interviewed in this study were married though the majority hoped to be one day. Most of these people expressed some doubts as to whether or not they would be able to, indeed for several this was a very real worry. Those who were married had met their partners at St Loye's or, in one case, at a PHAB club. Given the restricted social life and leisure activities of most of these young people the opportunities for making friends and meeting partners were few and far between. There seems to be a consensus of opinion that independence is a good thing that all young people should aim for, yet the discussion is often limited only to physical independence, while the rather more thought-provoking issue of emotional independence is ignored. A number of the young people in this study exhibited personal problems of a severe nature. Two young men were known to have attempted suicide, one young man saw himself as unpleasant and working through his bad feelings for all the taunts that had been made at him at school. Another spoke of his struggles to cope with his aggression and yet another of his great distaste for many of the authority figures he had encountered as a teenager. Professionals involved with disabled young people may feel that already by 16 some are developing an 'oddness', with the mannerisms and manner that demarcate them from the rest of society. Mona O'Moore (1980), in a study of children in school found that physically handicapped children in ordinary schools were not as well accepted by their peers as able-bodied children were, and suggested that certain components of emotional adjustment (i.e. sense of personal worth, sense of personal freedom and a feeling of belonging) and extraversion were factors influencing the readiness with which a physically handicapped child was accepted. Younghusband (op.cit.) suggested that how a child feels about himself and his handicap is a much more potent factor in determining his personal and social adjustment than the nature or even degree of his disability.

Clearly there may be significant difficulties to overcome for a young person with a physical disability. A social worker at one of the specialist colleges recalled how one day a young woman with spina bifida had come into her office immobilized, on a trolley. Apparently she had had a 'face like thunder'. During and after their talk the social worker had puzzled as to where she had seen an expression like that before. Then she remembered. She had worked some years ago, with 'disturbed' adolescent girls in a residential setting and that look was the one they had just before they ran away. How, she had pondered, do you run away when you are disabled? Disabled young people may benefit not only from counselling and discussion in the general issues affecting them as adolescents, but in the more individual personal dilemmas they may encounter. The young people's comments on such issues are discussed in Chapter Seven.

Social interaction – skills and difficulties

The young people who completed the questionnaire were asked to complete a self-rating scale of social interaction skills. They were asked to rate themselves on a scale from 0–4 for each of 13 situations, where 0 indicated that they had no difficulty, 1 slight difficulty, 2 moderate difficulty, 3 great difficulty and 4 that they would avoid the situation if possible. The scoring and the situations were selected from the work of Trower *et al.* (1978). Three of the respondents did not complete this section, so figures are available for 150 young people. An opportunity to meet some of them and to gain an impression of the reliability of the self-rating was provided by the interviews. Scores obtained from the questionnaire seemed to be accurate though it was felt that young people may have rather under-stated their difficulties.

Ninety-three per cent of the respondents rated themselves as having some difficulty in the social situations listed. Ratings of moderate or greater difficulty were made by 73 per cent of the respondents in, on average, four to five situations. Ratings of great difficulty or avoidance were made by 56 per cent of the respondents in an average of three situations. Indeed, there were 18 respondents who reported great difficulty or avoidance in as many as five or more situations and this 12 per cent of young people could be seen as suffering from a quite severe social handicap. A range of disabilities was represented in this last group, though those with hearing impairment or communication disorders were over-represented in that there were three people who were hearing impaired and three who had aphasia. Also included in this group were people with spina bifida, heart disorders, epilepsy and visual impairment. Details of the number of people scoring moderate difficulty or more for each of the 13 situations are given in Table 5.1.

It is of interest that the situations that were seen as most difficult by this group of young people are those concerned with social interactions where the personal risk might be considered greatest. The difficulties expressed with approaching others, keeping a conversation going, entertaining and talking about yourself may go some way to explain the social isolation of the majority of those interviewed. Nearly a quarter of the respondents stated that they had great difficulty in or would avoid situations where they needed to take the initiative and keep a conversation going and a fifth felt similarly about approaching others and making the first move to starting up a friendship. In view of the latter finding and the social isolation of most of the interviewees the relatively low scoring for the question about making friends of similar age seems surprising. It may be that this reflects a denial of a difficulty in the face of little opportunity to test the skill. One's inability to take the initiative, approach others and talk about oneself may be viewed with more clarity.

Table 5.1: Percentage of respondents scoring (a) moderate difficulty (2) and (b) great difficulty or avoidance (3, 4) in 13 situations

	% scoring moderate difficulty	*% scoring great difficulty or avoidance*
Taking the initiative and keeping a conversation going	15	23
Approaching others – making the first move and starting up a friendship	17	21
Talking about yourself and your feelings in a conversation	13	19
Going into a room full of people	9	17
Looking at people directly in the eyes	10	16
Making ordinary decisions affecting other (e.g. what to do in the evening)	15	14
People looking at you	14	13
Meeting strangers	15	12
Going out with someone you are attracted to	21	11
Being with a group containing both men and women of roughly the same age as you	9	8
Making friends of your own age	13	7
Mixing with people at work/college	7	1

These findings would seem to indicate a need for a structured programme of social skills training for young people in the Further Education Unit including specialist help for those with physical barriers to communication. Argyle (1967) reflects that 'social skills training would make it possible to raise the whole quality of normal social behaviour so that it is more efficient and more enjoyable, and results in help, co-operation and trust rather than rejection, misunderstanding and social barriers'. These three negative features of social interaction may occur more frequently for disabled young people as has already been discussed in this chapter which makes such a programme more immediately relevant to their lives than to those of their able-bodied peers. An improvement in social interaction skills may have implications not only for the personal and social life of young people but for their ability to obtain and retain employment. There were, for example, two hearing impaired young women who had had difficulties at work. One of them was said, by her employer, to have tantrums and another was described as 'very conscientious, but there are times where I feel that her shyness together with her disability can cause a problem in communicating. . .' Another young woman who has cerebral palsy was said to be lacking in confidence to such a degree that four months of her six months work experience placement had been taken up with gradually restoring her confidence. Another young man was said by his employer to need social skills training, though his work was satisfactory.

Some points raised in this chapter are summarized below.

- The concept of stigma and the tendency to group all disabled people together with an emphasis on their disability rather than their individuality was discussed. The confusion and ill-informed opinions that many able-bodied people express create particular problems for disabled people.

- The desire expressed by young people in this study to be treated as 'normal' human beings was commented on and the skills that they could usefully learn in order to manage their interactions with able-bodied people were mentioned. Able-bodied people may respond inappropriately in unfamiliar encounters with disabled people and a disabled person has to be able to deal with this and sometimes with unpleasantness.

- The social isolation of many of the young people was commented upon and it was suggested that many of them were able to mix socially when given suitable opportunities.

- Most people did not structure their time – membership of clubs and organizations was limited as was attendance at evening classes – and many were dissatisfied with their social life.

- Most of the interviewees were living with their parents and many expressed dissatisfaction with doing so, either because of their immediate or long-term concerns. The need for young people to gain a degree of independence was discussed.

- The need for emotional independence was stressed and the personal problems of some of the young people in this study were mentioned. Comment was made on the role that counselling could play.

- The scores of the young people who rated their own social interaction skills suggest that there are areas of interaction that could usefully be included in a programme of social skills training.

- Training may be of considerable benefit to the 12 per cent of young people who rated themselves as having quite severe social handi-cap and could ease the social and vocational development of many of the others.

CHAPTER SIX

Reflections on St Loye's

The questionnaire sent out to the young people in this study included a number of questions that provided an opportunity for them to comment on their time at St Loye's and to give their opinions and ideas. Many of them gave considerable time and thought to their responses. Gerber and Griffiths (1980) suggested, with reference to young people with cerebral palsy, that although much planning is done for them very rarely are the young people themselves asked what they think of the services provided. They felt that reviews of educational and vocational programmes by the recipients are beneficial in assessing what has worked, what has been of no value and what goals are most appropriate. The information detailed in this chapter supports the argument presented in Chapter Seven of the need for, and benefits of, post-school education for disabled school leavers and indicates some useful ways in which future developments could go.

Satisfaction with college life

Respondents were asked about how they had felt whilst at St Loye's and were given a choice of four answers ranging from 'Happy most of the time' to 'Unhappy most of the time'. A large majority – 69 per cent – felt that they had been happy most of the time, indeed one young man had added a fifth answer of his own stating that they were 'The happiest days of my life'. Twenty-four per cent of the young people felt that they had been happy some of the time, four per cent unhappy some of the time and three per cent unhappy most of the time. For the ten young people in the last two groupings, home-sickness was usually given as a reason.

Eighty-four per cent of the respondents gave at least one reason why they had felt as they had and several of them gave a very comprehensive answer including three or four points. The percentage of young people giving each reason is given in Table 6.1.

Table 6.1: Comments on satisfaction with time spent in the Further Education Unit (n=129)

Reason	% of young people
Enjoyable social life	47
Pleasant atmosphere	19
Helpful staff	14
Contact with other disabled people	11
Plenty to do	11
Negative comments about staff or residential life	19
Opportunity for personal development	7
Enjoyed the work	15
Other	23

The most frequently given reason was the enjoyable social life and the opportunity to make friends, which was given by 47 per cent of the young people answering this question. One young woman wrote that she had 'plenty of company and friends – enjoyed working also plenty of social life'. A young man enjoyed his time in the Unit as he 'had a lot of friends, went interesting places, was made at home and had a good time'. One striking aspect of this opportunity for friendship was mentioned by several respondents.

Peter is a friendly, rather nervous young man who suffers from epilepsy and eczema. He attended a comprehensive school before entering St Loye's where he followed four terms of further education with the Store-keeping course. He wrote 'I was happy most of the time because I came with a good batch of people and I was going out with a girl called Sue and no one took the mickey.out of anyone else, because we all had a disability'. During his interview Peter spoke of his realization on his assessment day that 'People weren't going to make fun of your disability' and recalled telling his mother when he arrived home, 'I've got to go there'.

Another young man from a comprehensive school provided an insight into what attendance at a specialist college can entail when he wrote of being with his 'own people who knew what my feelings was, people who were in the same boat as me'. The phrase 'in the same boat' was in fact used by several of the respondents to refer to other disabled people. Eleven per cent of the young people mentioned explicitly the opportunities they had had to mix with other disabled people though this may have been implicit in many of the comments about the social life and the atmosphere. For example, John wrote 'Because I made friends there. It was a very pleasant atmosphere. Everybody got on with one and another'. In all but one case this was seen as a positive feature. Some people felt that they had come to realize that there were people worse off than themselves and had had the chance to see how other people coped with their disabilities.

The quotations above illustrate one important aspect of specialist provision. It may provide an opportunity for disabled young people to form an identity and to gain from peer group support – an opportunity that may be denied them in the normal course of events. Some of the parents of these young people mentioned the camaradarie they had seen at the college and were pleased that their son or daughter had had the chance to take part. One mother described how moved she was by the effort many of the young people made each year to travel back to college for the Fete to meet up with their friends. Against this must be balanced the risk of labelling young people unnecessarily.

Graham is a young man mildly handicapped with spina bifida in that only his neck and shoulders are affected. He attended the local comprehensive school before going to St Loye's and explained, during his interview that he had never really seen himself as disabled until it had been suggested that he apply to St Loye's.

Labelling may also have consequences that go beyond the self-image. Three young people spoke, during their interviews of the negative change in people's attitudes when they realize that you had been to a college for disabled people. One felt that it had affected her chances of obtaining employment and another that his search for accommodation had been made considerably more difficult. Another comment was made by a man with spina bifida who wrote that he 'didn't like being amongst disabilities you could see where you all stick out like a sore thumb away from college when you went out'. Oswin (op.cit.) writes of the way in which disabled adolescents may feel 'safer' with each other and out of things with their families and non-handicapped people and speaks of the intense friendships that can be formed in a residential setting. She does however stress that young people need to be equipped to cope with life in the community, to be able to obtain and keep a job and to get on with other young people.

A frequent comment referred to the general atmosphere of the college which 19 per cent of the young people mentioned. Some people wrote of the friendly relaxed atmosphere, others referred to the college as a pleasant place to be. A further 11 per cent referred to the opportunities for keeping oneself occupied. As one young man said simply 'so much to do'. Fourteen per cent of the respondents to this question made positive comments about staff. Several of the young people described them as 'kind and helpful' and similar comments were made by those people interviewed. Some young people said that they were still in touch with members of staff and they visit them when they have an opportunity. One particular teacher's patience and understanding were remembered by several of the interviewees. One respondent wrote 'They gave me help with my maths and English, because they understood my problem'. Another wrote that '. . . I felt more confident and able to do more because I was encouraged and helped through the course by the friends I made and the staff'.

Half of the negative responses about staff or residential life referred to the respondents' homesickness. One young woman wrote 'I was extremely home-sick at first. Also my mum had only just died. I would have been much happier if I'd had the chance of a room of my own to sleep'. Ben felt that he was 'rather young and immature to be so far from home' and Lucy that she missed her family and 'went back home every week-end, didn't want to go back'. A few comments in this group referred to difficulties in getting on with other residents, as in the case of one young man who complained that some 'troublemakers' didn't like his hobbies. Most of the negative comments made about staff were either that young people felt that they were treated as

children rather than as young adults, or that the rules on the residential side were inappropriate. There have been significant changes in
the latter in recent years; indeed some of the young people who had
kept in touch with the College tempered their criticism by commenting
favourably on such changes.

Comments about staff were also made when respondents were
asked about what changes, if any, they would make if they were running the Further Education Unit and what they had enjoyed most
when they were there. Fourteen per cent of the respondents to the
latter question (there were 179 responses from 140 young people)
wrote about the staff. One young man suggested that 'the instructors
were prepared to go into great depth if you didn't understand any
aspect of the course', and another that 'the thing I enjoyed most about
the FE was the way things were explained to you, the way the tutors
treated you as an individual'. One young woman had enjoyed 'Having the teachers there and knowing they could put more time to you
and your work and explaining things to you as there wasn't so many to
attend to like there was at school'. A number of young people commented favourably on the high staff/student ratio. As regards changes
(there were 137 suggestions from 120 young people) 13 per cent of the
young people made suggestions about staff attitudes – again 'treat us
more like adults than children' was a typical response.

With regard to people's responses as to why they had felt as they
had while at St Loye's a further 15 per cent replied that it was because
they had enjoyed the work and seven per cent that it had helped them
to develop personally, for example – 'I used to be very quiet and shy
but going to St Loye's helped me to come out of my shell.' The remaining responses provided a wide variety of reasons. One visually-
handicapped young man felt that he had attended the wrong college
as his particular disorder is not catered for at St Loye's and claimed to
have been unhappy some of the time. A young woman felt that she
was happy most of the time especially during the first two terms, but
not very happy in the third term when she realized that a 'suitable job
was most unlikely to occur after training'. One young man who had
been unemployed for the 22 months since leaving college had been
happy most of the time because he thought it would help him to find
employment. Another who had worked for three weeks in the 30
months since leaving college, before being made redundant, felt that
he had been happy for most of the time because 'I had something to
look forward to, the chance of a job, but after my second month in the

trainees (the adult training course) I was terminated owing to my health. I wasn't given any hints about the fact that I was slipping in my paper work'.

Suggestions for change

Suggestions for changes that related to staff have already been discussed. Thirty-three per cent of the young people who answered this question suggested changes that would prepare them for employment, 18 per cent suggested changes to the curriculum and 23 per cent wrote that they couldn't think of anything that could make the Unit better. One young woman's very full answer sums up typical responses in that she mentioned work experience, lectures on industrial relations, choice about doing games and advice on looking after yourself and your home. The percentage of young people suggesting each change is given in Table 6.2.

Table 6.2: Suggestions for change (n=120)

Change	% of young people
Employment related	33
Curriculum	18
Couldn't make it better	23
Staff attitudes	13
Other '	28

Comments were made both about helping students to find work through such means as mock interviews – 'So that we can be told our faults' – and about preparing young people for the reality of work. One young woman suggested, 'Tell them what is expected of them when they do start work, tell them it is not always good, sometimes they will have to sort out some bad times'. She had been employed for 74 per cent of the time since leaving St Loye's, on a Youth Opportunities Programme that had lasted for six months and then in a job that had lasted for 11 months before she was made redundant. This last point about preparation for work is in line with the proposals made in an Industrial Training Research Unit report (1979) which suggests that young employees should be introduced 'to a range of experiences and problems relevant to adult working life, coupled with guidance in interpreting and dealing with critical situations' and that 'to "teach" in the areas where these young people could benefit, that is, in developing and harnessing useful personal qualities opens up an entirely new training area'.

The Work Preparation course, discussed in the Introduction, was mentioned by some people. As one young man suggested, 'St Loye's had a course in the last term that was designed to help people leaving. The course was quite good, but should be more detailed in areas to do with where to look for work'. A young woman wrote '. . . At one time people who had to leave straight after the FE Unit because they failed their course assessment were given very little to hope for, but now a woman is employed to help those who have to leave early to find jobs which is a very good idea'.

One young man suggested that work experience was useful in enabling 'the candidate to get to grips with his situation' and that this was especially important because 'employers must be taught to judge disabled people by their skill not their inherent physical or physiological disorder'. Another young man would advise young people 'on how to approach an employer and (on which) people to try and approach who could help you in finding employment'. Barry suggested that it would have been useful to have been shown how to deal with forms. He had filled in a claim form when unemployed and said that 'I filled one in at the Social Security and didn't have a clue, just put anything down, didn't like their attitude. It's soul-destroying, you go into an office, don't know anybody, offices don't have time for you, could do it there (St Loye's)'. One young man provided a comprehensive answer. 'I would ask the student what kind of career they would like to embark on and then have the Youth Employment Officer (careers officer) talk to them to advise them on what type of exams you would have to have and to advise them on the jobs available in the district in which you live. Have time available for the student to try out the kind of work he/she would be doing and then talk to them again'.

Clearly, although 26 per cent of respondents answered that their time in the Further Education Unit had given them a very useful idea of what it was like living and working in the adult world and 46 per cent felt it had given them a quite useful idea, there were ways in

which some young people felt changes could be made. These suggestions are based on their experience of looking for and, in some cases,
obtaining employment.

As regards changes to the curriculum, several people felt that they
would have liked the opportunity and more encouragement to take
examinations for, as one young man wrote, 'These open doors to
employment'. GCE (General Certificate of Education) exams were
mentioned by some people. These may be unrealistic aims for many of
the young people at the college, and the RSA (Royal Society of Arts)
Certificates taken by some students are regarded as more relevant to
their future employment. One young woman stressed the need for
training to 'keep up with the times' and a young man would have liked
'more realistic working conditions'. With regard to the structure of
the day another would have liked to 'change the timetables so that the
students spend more time doing one particular kind of work because
when I was there I found it more like school with only an hour or so at
one subject'. Another would change the hours of work to a normal
working day.

Of the young people who wrote that they couldn't think of any
changes they would make, a few were adamant that there weren't any
changes that could be an improvement. One young man felt that 'I
couldn't make any changes at all. They do a wonderful job and I'm
proud to say to anyone that I attended St Loye's College'. This pride
and enthusiasm with which some of the young people remember their
time at St Loye's was evident during the interviews. Several young
people had framed their diplomas and displayed them on living-room
walls.

Apart from the suggestions already discussed the respondents
made a number of miscellaneous comments such as 'employ more
teachers for the deaf', 'involve able-bodied people more' and 'prepare
one for people's attitudes outside when you say you are disabled.
They group mental disability and physical disability together'. One
young man would wish to 'Take notice of how the student sees his
future and not condemn ambition too readily' and another would 'Let
them have more say in the type of work they are going to end up doing
for the rest of their life'. One young man had been employed as a
general catering assistant all the time since leaving St Loye's and had
added a post-script to his questionnaire 'I would also like to thank
everybody at St Loye's for getting me where I am today'. His response
to the question about suggestions for change was 'I would try to make

the place bigger with more classrooms so that they could get more people in and help them'.

Has it been worthwhile?

The respondents to the questionnaire were also asked whether or not they felt, looking back, that it had been worth their while to take the Further Education Course. Five people did not answer and of those that did 86 per cent felt that it had been so. In view of the emphasis often given to the enhancement of employment prospects as a result of further education, it could be anticipated that the young people's retrospective perceptions of the value of the course would be coloured by their employment history and current employment status. This however was not the case. Eighty-eight per cent of the young people who had had open employment felt that the course had been worth it, but so did 82 per cent of those who had not been so employed. Eighty-nine per cent of the young people currently in open employment were positive about the value of the course, as were 83 per cent of those currently not in open employment. The reasons why people felt that the course had been worthwhile or not are given in Table 6.3.

Table 6.3: Reasons why the course was or was not worthwhile (n=134)

Reason	% of young people
Opportunity to learn	46
Helped with employment/ training	20
Personal development	18
Other	13
No better off	11

The most commonly mentioned reason why the course had been worthwhile was that it had been an opportunity to learn and indeed 46 per cent of the young people answering gave this as a reason. One young person felt that it 'filled in most of the gaps from school', another that 'I think I learnt more whilst on the Further Education course than I had learnt in my last few years at school', and another that 'I didn't have much of an education, so when I went to college I learnt more in that short time than I had ever learnt'. Some of the responses indicated why there had been this educational gain mentioning their absences from school because of their illness, the quality of education they had received at school and the small classes and individual attention at St Loye's.

One young man had felt that it was worth his while to take the course, indeed he had added, 'Very much so' to his answer explaining that 'I learnt more at St Loye's than in my whole school life, maybe because my attitude had changed and (I) realised its importance'. Another, currently employed in a sheltered workshop, felt that 'Although I did not do very well there I feel I learned quite a lot more'. Sometimes comments were qualified as with the young woman who wrote 'Well, some of the work seemed repetitive after school, but looking back I probably needed the revision, especially in maths, that was very useful'.

The next most commonly given reason was that the course had helped in finding employment or had provided training for employment and 20 per cent of the young people wrote of this. One young man wrote that 'It gets you prepared for assessment to pass on to a course in the workshops or the rest of the college'. One young woman felt that the course would help her 'to obtain better employment' and another that it had built up her typing speeds and taught her the clerical duties she is doing now. A further 18 per cent of the young people felt that the course had helped them to develop independence or other personal attributes that were seen as desirable. One young man felt that 'It broadened my outlook' and another that 'It helped me to grow up'. Yet another provided a particularly full answer, writing of how much he had learnt and of the personal attention he had received adding that 'it gave me the chance of being independent, doing my own ironing and washing, etc., it therefore was a great chance which proved that if I wished to live on my own or was forced to move away from home for one reason or another that I could manage without anyone's help'.

Thirteen per cent of the young people gave one of a variety of reasons why the course had been worthwhile ranging from 'Every little helps' to 'because I passed my first two exams' to 'I found afterwards that I had no hesitation to ask for help'. In addition there were some people who felt that the course had been worthwhile, but who qualified their answer and some 11 per cent who gave a reason why they felt that the course had not been worth their while. In the former grouping one young woman felt 'But the classes were too big for me because of my deafness and it was not possible for the teacher to explain the various points to me', and another that it had been worth while 'Because of the people I met, not particularly because of the course itself'. One young man who had replied positively then went on to say 'But not at St Loye's, stating that he had moved on to another specialist college.

Of the young people who gave a reason as to why the course had not been worth their while some felt that they had not learnt much, as with this young woman who felt that 'Everything they were teaching me I already knew from school which I left a few weeks before starting' and some that their time could have been better spent looking for work. One young man who had gone on to the Horticulture course and who had been unemployed for all but three weeks of the 2½ years since leaving felt that 'Because in the end (I) had wasted around two years of my life, time which I could have used looking for a job'. Again some answers were qualified. One young man gave a negative answer adding 'Because it has not really helped me get a job, although I do not regret the time spent there'. Another person felt that although the course had not been worth her while she had learnt a lot that had helped her in her course at the local technical college.

What was most enjoyable, useful or not?

Respondents to the questionnaire were asked what they enjoyed most about the Further Education course and 140 of the young people replied, providing 179 answers between them. The most frequently given answer was the social life and opportunity for social development which was mentioned by 30 per cent of them. As one young man wrote 'Learning to get on with other people'. Literacy and numeracy were classified separately from the other courses and 16 per cent of the young people felt that these two courses had been the most enjoyable. The other courses provided were mentioned by 28 per cent of the young people and a general comment about the opportunity to learn was made by 15 per cent of respondents. Positive comments about the staff were made by 14 per cent and 26 per cent of them gave one of a number of miscellaneous replies.

Of those people classified as having enjoyed their social life most, some had stated 'the company' and others had written 'meeting people'. Miscellaneous comments covered a wide area. A young person who had done the Work Preparation course enjoyed 'Learning how to work out a wage packet and also looking at films about jobs', another 'the feeling of heading for a brighter future', another meeting her husband-to-be and another receiving a diploma. One young man enjoyed the feeling of being 'more capable to cope with life better as the weeks fly by'.

When asked what they had found most useful about the Further Education course the various courses were mentioned by the majority of respondents. One hundred and twenty-seven people replied providing 149 answers. Twenty-seven per cent of the young people mentioned literacy and numeracy as being the most useful aspect of the course, while 26 per cent made a general comment about their educational progress. One young man wrote 'I found that learning could be fun', and a young woman felt that it had kept her up to date with the work 'just like other youngsters of my age'. Thirteen per cent mentioned the commercial skills they had acquired and the same percentage mentioned advances in their personal development. In this latter group one young woman wrote of starting to be independent, facing life better with her disability, not being so conscious of it and standing up for herself. A young man enjoyed working on his own, using his initiative and gaining independence. Ten per cent mentioned the technical training and two per cent wrote of general studies. A large proportion, 27 per cent, gave one of a variety of reasons. These included, 'Having little jobs to do in the evenings and prefect duties and organising bath rotas', 'the course was so much different from school', 'the availability of tools and machinery at hand which otherwise I would not have been able to use until at work', and 'I can't really point out any one thing. My brain at last decided it wanted to learn'. The young man who had done the Work Preparation course felt that 'experience in job interviews, understanding job advertisements' and learning 'how to go about applying for a job' were the most useful aspects of the course.

Finally, the young people were asked whether there was anything they think they would rather have not done on the Further Education course. One hundred and eighteen of the young people answered this and 65 per cent of them said that there wasn't anything. Of those that did give a positive answer, six per cent mentioned games, nine per cent general studies, nine per cent the technical training and one per cent the commercial. The young people who would rather have not done technical skills were mainly people who had gone on to a commercial training after the Further Education course. One young woman wrote that she would rather not have done 'the technical work, e.g. wiring seemed a bit of a waste but I suppose I must have had to go into something like that if I hadn't passed my telephonist's/typing assessment'. As regards games one visually handicapped young woman wrote '. . . although I like sport, I was very embarrassed at not being able to see'. Games lessons are no longer part of the curriculum in the Further Education Unit. One of the people who wrote of general studies felt that she 'would rather have had more English or maths'. Again there was a range of miscellaneous answers including 'English' and 'not have been in a class like school again'. The comments made in response to the last three questions are given in Table 6.4.

Table 6.4: Comments on what was most enjoyable, useful or not

	Comment	% of young people
Most enjoyable (n=140)		
	Social life/development	30
	Literacy and numeracy	16
	Other courses	28
	Opportunity to learn	15
	Staff	14
	Other	26
Most useful (n=127)		
	Literacy and numeracy	27
	Opportunity to learn	26
	Commercial skills	13
	Personal and social development	13
	Technical skills	10
	General studies	2
	Other	27
Rather not have done (n=118)		
	No, everything was useful	65
	Games	6
	General studies	9
	Technical	9
	Commercial	1
	Other	10

The main points from this chapter are summarized below.

- The majority of young people felt that they had been happy most of the time whilst in the Further Education Unit. The most frequently given reason for this was the opportunity to make friends and to have an enjoyable social life. A specialist college may provide young people with the chance to gain from peer group support at this important stage in their development.

- When asked what changes they would make to the Further Education Unit, 33 per cent of the young people suggested changes that would prepare them for employment. Visits to work places, work experience, mock interviews, careers guidance and placing help were all mentioned.

- Eighty-eight per cent of the young people who had had open employment felt that it had been worth their while to take the Further Education course, as did 82 per cent of those who had not been so employed. Perceptions of the usefulness of the course were not coloured either by employment history or current employment status.

- The most frequently given reason why the course had been worthwhile was that it had provided a valuable opportunity to learn. The benefits obtained from small classes and individual attention were mentioned by several people.

- Of the 14 per cent of young people who did not feel that the course had been worthwhile most felt that they had not learnt much from it or that their time could have been better spent looking for employment.

- Literacy and numeracy skills were specifically mentioned by 27 per cent of the young people as being the most useful aspect of the course. Indeed 16 per cent had found them the most enjoyable part. Gains in these basic skills may have been implicit in many of the comments about opportunities to learn.

CHAPTER SEVEN

Developing their Capabilities and Skills to the Maximum?

In the United Nations General Assembly of December 1979 a 13-point Declaration of the Rights of Disabled Persons was approved and it was anticipated that such a declaration would provide a common international basis and frame of reference for the protection of those rights. 1981 was officially designated as the International Year of Disabled People. There are two points in the declaration that are particularly relevant to the issues raised in this report and they are quoted in full below.

'Disabled persons have the right to medical, psychological and functional treatment, including prosthetic and orthotic appliances, to medical and social rehabilitation, education, vocational education, training and rehabilitation, aid, counselling, placement services and other services which will enable them to develop their capabilities and skills to the maximum and will hasten the process of their social integration or reintegration.'

'Disabled persons have the right to economic and social security and to a decent level of living. They have the right, according to their capabilities, to secure and retain employment or to engage in a useful, productive and remunerative occupation and to join trade unions.'

Meeting the need

In the Warnock Report (op.cit.) the importance of post-school education and training for young people with special needs was emphasized. Considerable evidence had been submitted to the Committee stressing the need for education to be available to young people with disabilities or significant difficulties beyond the age of 16. It was reported that there were 15,000 handicapped 15-year-olds in full-time education, 6,000 16-year-olds and only 1,000 17-year-olds. The National Children's Bureau Study commissioned by Warnock showed that five times as many able-bodied young people were still in full-time education at the age of 18 years compared with handicapped young people. Younghusband (op.cit.) suggested '. . . many who work with handicapped adolescents are convinced that they experience an acceleration in maturation after 16. In later years of adolescence many severely handicapped young people make progress at an increased rate provided these years are passed in an appropriate educational setting'.

In an assessment of the need for further education and training for handicapped school-leavers Tuckey *et al.* (1973) found that 83 per cent of the young people in their study were considered suitable for further education and/or training by their headteachers. However only a third of those considered suitable for further education with or without training actually received it. The study only dealt with leavers from special schools and further education was loosely defined to include, for example, attendance at evening and adult literacy classes. Two-thirds of the young people in their study were from schools for educationally sub-normal (ESN) pupils, nearly one in five from those for physically handicapped children and one in ten from those for visually or hearing impaired children. Even taking their broad definition of further education, only 40 per cent of the physically-handicapped young people, 20 per cent of those with epilepsy, 23 per cent of those who were deaf and partially-hearing and 47 per cent of the partially-sighted leavers received such education. Given these findings and the more recent concerns expressed by Warnock (op.cit.) it seems clear that there is insufficient provision for this group of young people. As Warnock (op.cit.) suggested 'We recognise that relatively few young people with disabilities or significant difficulties have achieved by the age of 16 either their full educational potential or an adequate degree of maturity to make a smooth transition to adult life. . . Educational provision must therefore be far more widely available to such young people beyond the age of 16'. Oswin (op.cit.) writes that 'If disabled young people do not get help with further education and training, then it is very easy for them to feel useless and unwanted'.

Given the overall lack of provision another matter of concern is the procedure by which young people are referred to specialist colleges. A visit by a member of college staff to his or her part of the country, a change in personnel in the local Careers Office or an informed and motivated parent may all influence significantly the chances a disabled young person has of being referred to a specialist college. Nath (personal communication) in a study of young people with cerebral palsy found that those people who had had a Spastics Society assessment were substantially more likely to have had residential further education than those who had not. She studied two groups of young people matched in terms of variables such as sex, IQ and area of residence and differing in that only one group had had the assessment.

Local education authority provisions for disabled school-leavers are discussed in other literature, for example, Panckhurst (1980) and Rowan (op.cit.). Cuts in spending on education may severely restrict the discretionary awards available from local authorities and residential provision which is funded by such awards may be offered to even fewer young people. Financial restrictions may also limit the amount of in-county development of provision for disabled school-leavers. At the present time (academic year 1981/2) some local education authorities may be turning to residential provision in a period of high youth unemployment if their restrictions on out-of-county expenditure are not prohibitive, whereas other areas may be experiencing severe cut-backs.

> *Mr and Mrs Fox, the parents of one young man interviewed, were eager to learn of how other young people had come to hear of St Loye's. As their son, Nigel, approached school-leaving age they had been concerned as to what he should do and when Mrs Fox visited the village shop one day she voiced her concern. A fellow shopper had mentioned the son of some friends of hers who had gone to St Loye's and a meeting with these friends was arranged. The parents took up Nigel's case from there, armed with the knowledge that such a college existed.*

One young interviewee had been told of four other places he could have applied to and seemed to have been given a fair amount of information, making the choice of St Loye's himself, because it was the nearest. His case was not however typical. Many young people felt that they had not had a choice about where they went and that the decision had been made for them. As one young man suggested 'I was on the side-lines, they were running the game, they suggested it and I thought they were older and wiser'. One mother interrupted when her daughter was asked about her decision to go to St Loye's claiming 'You don't get a choice when you have handicapped children, that's the attitude, you don't have any choice'.

One of Warnock's (op.cit.) recommendations was that '. . . the national colleges which currently provide further education or training for young people with disabilities should in time all become part of their regional patterns of further education for students with special needs' and certainly such provision would help to alleviate some of the short-comings of the present system. This development was also recommended by the Regional Advisory Council for the Organization of Further Education in the East Midlands (1981) who emphasized the need for co-operation and co-ordination regionally in further education and stressed the importance of expanding provision making it available for all those who wish it. Their publication 'Further Education for Handicapped People 1980–81' gives a comprehensive account of colleges in the region in terms of their specialist facilities, specialist teaching and non-teaching staff and specialist course provision. Local education authorities do have an obligation, though this is sometimes over-looked, to provide all young people who want it with continued full-time education between the ages of 16–19 either in school or in a further education establishment.

Most of the young people in this study had not even considered attending local educational provision, though for some this may well have been possible and indeed desirable. A few young people felt they would not have been able to cope with the courses they thought were available at their local college and some mentioned reactions to their disability. One young man who had attended a special school felt that he would have been uneasy about going to an ordinary college as 'people would look at me and think "he's disabled" and take the mick'. He added 'I'm a shy person and don't fight for myself'. One young woman had been unable to train as a telephonist locally as she could not mount the steep steps up to the college in her wheelchair and would not have been able to reach the standard switch-boards provided. Access problems and adaptations to equipment need not be insurmountable restrictions and as Warnock (op.cit.) suggests '. . . in many cases the most important factor will be the attitude of staff '. A small number of people in fact attended courses in local colleges after leaving St Loye's.

One specialist college visited during this study had made arrangements for students considered suitable to attend the local technical college on a day-release basis, thereby benefiting from the course and receiving back-up support from the college. Other specialist colleges may find this facility a useful way of allowing students to keep in touch with the wider community. Colleges for disabled people may too easily be regarded, and experienced, as enclaves. The policy of staff at St Loye's to encourage local young people to socialize in the Further Education Unit one evening a week was commented on spontaneously by many of the young people interviewed and indicates the importance of both reaching out to and drawing in from the local community. One young man described as 'fantastic' the times he and other young people at St Loye's had gone to a local college of education for sports coaching. He had been really impressed by the fact that trainee teachers had bothered to coach 'people like me when they are so fit and healthy'.

The residential specialist colleges can provide young people with an opportunity to gain some independence, to learn in small groups, to mix with their disabled peers and to benefit from the experience of staff used to dealing with a variety of special needs. These facilities could, given sufficient resources, be made available to young people on a regional basis. The difficulties of implementing plans for a regional pattern of further education for students with special needs were discussed by Panckhurst and McAllister (1980). It was suggested that 'colleges with national coverage might be encouraged to continue their work, perhaps in innovative and experimental ways, and to put back into further education as a whole – through courses and publication – some of the insights and knowledge they have acquired'.

Greaves and Massie (op.cit.) found that many disablement resettlement officers they spoke to felt that a major difficulty in finding work was that many disabled people did not have the necessary skills to do the job. As they suggest, more thought should be given to training and preparing disabled people for work and obviously colleges such as St Loye's are fulfilling an important role. Training and education will not, by themselves, find disabled people suitable jobs, but without them there will never be an opportunity for them to overcome the disadvantage already imposed by their disability. There is a con-

sensus of opinion in the relevant literature and among many professionals working in the field that education and training are essential
for disabled school-leavers. However, a system whereby so many
chance factors determine whether or not an application is made to a
specialist college, where young people who could usefully attend local
provision are debarred because of access problems or are not even
considered eligible to apply and where so few places are available cannot be considered to be meeting the need.

Identifying the need

Another related issue is that of assessment. The policy at St Loye's is
to make recommendations for each of the approximately 40 per cent of
applicants they do not offer a place to. Recommendations are sent
back to the careers officer and may well result in a successful placement. However for many of the young people who are not offered a
place this 'rejection' may be extremely disheartening. Clearly, many
of the young people interviewed saw their offer of a place as a measure
of their 'success' on the assessment day. An assessment by an independent group of professionals at an appropriate time in a young
person's school career would alleviate this possible distress and an
assessment of longer duration would counter the sometimes scanty
information available about young people, and their nervousness on
the day. A more comprehensive assessment may also minimize the
loss of young people who start a course and then 'drop out'. Assessment, of course, works both ways and young people could avoid the
misunderstandings about the college which were sometimes expressed by those interviewed. One young man spoke of his surprise
when on starting his course at St Loye's it had been 'just like going
back to school' as he had expected to start training. Another had been
told by his careers officer that he could do painting and decorating at
St Loye's and it wasn't until he was some way through the further
education course that he realized he could not. There were two young
people excluded from this study as they had only stayed at the college
for two or three days and two who had not turned up at the beginning
of term.

The impact that value-laden, seemingly irreversible, comments on
young people's attainments, and personality can have was a matter of
concern to the social worker at another specialist college. She spoke of

application forms where negative or critical comments about applicants were often undated. Of particular importance for this group of young people is the accuracy of their medical reports. In a letter to the *Lancet* (1978) Dr David Elliman expressed his concern about the way in which a school-leaver's subsequent employment may be restricted by what is entered on his or her forms. He studied the reports of the seven young people with epilepsy who had had school leavers' medicals in the borough in which he was working and found that the comment on their forms 'In my opinion this pupil is not suitable for work at heights or near vehicles in action' was unfairly restrictive in three cases and needed reviewing in two others. Dr Elliman suggests that his review of these cases does raise a number of questions not the least of which is 'Are equally inappropriate restrictions being applied to children with other chronic conditions?'. Certainly one young man in this study felt that he had been unfairly labelled as having epilepsy even though he had only ever had convulsions as a baby.

The suggested assessments referred to above could most usefully be conducted in close collaboration with the various establishments in the region. A centralized source of information would be built up that could highlight possible curriculum developments and gaps in available provisions. Such assessments would be more costly than present arrangements but on the other side of the balance is the loss of potential already discussed in this chapter and the possibly inappropriate placing of young people at this crucial stage in their development.

Personal and social needs

Chapter Five discussed in detail the personal development and needs of the young people in this study and it seems appropriate here to consider whether changes in curriculum and resources could enhance their emotional and social functioning. There have been considerable changes in the residential provision at St Loye's since the majority of the young people in this study were there. A number of those interviewed who had visited the college since leaving commented favourably on the new residential building and wished that they too had had the luxury of a single or twin-bedded room. The present houseparents see themselves as having three main objectives: to boost the residents' confidence, to develop independence and to teach social and life skills. The houseparents' awareness of a need to provide more of a framework for the residents' free time is in line with current thinking elsewhere. As a recent Further Education Curriculum Review and Development Unit report (1980) suggests 'What is undeniable is that social education is now a live issue in further education'. This report suggests that one reason for the development of social education for young people is the Manpower Services Commission's recognition of the likely relevance of social competence to their work, and to their chances of gaining employment.

A recent paper (Department of Education and Science/Department of Employment, 1979) concerned with vocational preparation suggests social and life skills as one of the three areas which any scheme should aim to cover. Speake and Whelan (1979) asked occupational supervisors on work preparation courses for young people with special needs what they considered to be the main ways in which youngsters could develop in order to become ready for employment. The most frequently mentioned area was that of personality and personal characteristics such as maturity, learning to become more adult, accepting the limitations of their disability, thinking for oneself and having respect for others. Teachers on the courses provided answers that agreed closely with these. Growing awareness of the need to develop this aspect of young people's potential is indicated by the examinations in Communications offered by the Technician Education Council and by the City and Guilds of London Institute.

Such developments taking place in the education of able-bodied people are commendable though the need to develop this part of the curriculum for disabled young people may be more urgent, given the particular difficulties they may encounter. As John Hilbourne (1973) suggests 'It would be somewhat utopian to argue that their (disabled people's) lot can be considerably improved by public education'. He suggests that, as many problems arise from a misconception about the nature and consequences of disabilities among the general public, effort should be expended to enable disabled people to understand and cope with these, and disabled individuals should be given as much help as possible in the techniques they can use for structuring uncertain situations for other people'. The point is well made and Hilbourne's suggestions combined with a policy of public information and opportunities for disabled and able-bodied people to mix may go some way to ease the stigma attached to being disabled. Public education may be a long and difficult process but developments such as the recent advertisement by one City Council for a Disabled Persons'

Access Officer do indicate a certain awareness of the need.

The MSC's 'Instructional Guide to Social and Life Skills' (1980) provides a framework for such a programme though the problems involved need careful consideration. Working with new ideas which the staff are not specifically trained to deal with and which the students may not immediately see the relevance of may be difficult. An expansion of the social and life skills commitment at St Loye's may prove beneficial to future residents. Certainly many young people commented on changes they would have liked in terms of learning work-related skills rather than just how to do a particular job. The mother of one young hearing impaired woman felt that the emphasis the staff at St Loye's had put on doing the job well to earn good money could have been usefully supplemented by advice on how to behave at work, as she felt that her daughter had twice nearly lost her job by her inappropriate behaviour. A related difficulty was expressed by the colleagues of another hearing impaired young woman for, as one of them suggested, '. . . If from the beginning Eileen had been better at lip-reading her involvement and confidence would have been alright and her life and work so much more enjoyable'.

The perceptions and reflections of the young people in this study are detailed in Chapter Six, though one is relevant here. The respondents were asked whether or not there was any special help that they would have liked at St Loye's that they didn't have and were told that this could be educational, medical, personal or any other sort of help. Thirty-three per cent of those answering this question would have liked some help. There were some students who would have liked help because of their disability, for example the visually-handicapped young woman who would have liked to have been 'trained to handle the handicap I have', the hearing impaired young woman who would have liked help from 'a teacher who could do sign language for the deaf' and the young man who would have liked 'a resident physiotherapist, for general manipulation to keep my legs and feet supple'. Specialist help was requested by most of the young people with hearing impairment or communication disorders. Several people mentioned help in finding a job, more choice in what courses they did and the need for more information about their benefits and entitlements. One young man would have liked 'a general knowledge of what to expect if you can't get a job'.

A third of those who would have liked special help would have liked help of a personal sort. As one young woman suggested 'I found no one to talk over my troubles with, very little personal help when I needed it'. A young man would have liked 'a more easy atmosphere so that people could know that there was someone they could tell their problems to in confidence' and another thought that '. . . the personal side was a bit lax at times – someone who new students could turn to for advice and comfort'. Oswin (op.cit.) writes of the need of disabled adolescents for strong family support in order to give them some incentive to keep going. For those young people without familial support, help of a personal kind may be valuable.

The young people interviewed were asked how they would feel about having someone on the staff or coming in from outside who was there specially for students to talk over their personal worries with and the majority were positive in their response. One young woman felt that 'if personal problems are affecting your work, everything will go wrong'. Of those that did not feel a need for such support, the idea that you could go and chat to your friends about anything that was worrying you was a common response. This may be so for many young people, but it assumes not only that you are capable of making friendships of sufficient depth but also that you have made such friendships soon enough to be of use. The social worker at another specialist college held a discussion session where the young people were asked about stress in their lives. The majority of young people felt that the most stressful time in their lives so far had been their first two weeks at the college. As was suggested in Chapter Five, some young people had difficulties beyond the scope of those that could be talked out over a cup of coffee and needed more skilled help than that available from a peer. There would seem to be a need for consistent, personal help of a confidential and professionally qualified kind. Oswin (op.cit.) made reference to a social worker working with disabled adolescents who spoke of her concern as to 'who answers the questions of these adolescents who are out of touch with their families and who. . . . are going to have a lifelong handicap?' As Oswin suggests 'At present they have to find their own philosophy amongst their companions. . . .'

The role of parents

Another relevant issue is the role that parents have, and the relationship between parents and staff at the college. Parents may be anxious about their child being away from home at 16, particularly if the child's disability has made exceptional demands on them. Some parents may indeed feel a sense of loss that may exacerbate their concern. As was stated in the Introduction there were a few parents who felt unable to leave the interview that was intended for the young person. One mother of a 23-year-old hearing impaired young woman insisted on answering most of the questions for her daughter and said that she wouldn't let her daughter go back to any residential setting as she doesn't see why she should have to put up with the unpleasantness of being with other people. Closer co-operation between parents and staff may not only help to alleviate parents' concerns but may work to the advantage of the young person. One mother whose 23-year-old son had mild cerebral palsy complained of how he had come home from St Loye's with dirty hair, adding that 'everyone knows that boys won't wash unless they are made to'. What may have been an attempt to allow a measure of independence to a 16-year-old boy was not considered as such. Similarly, two young women with spina bifida when interviewed complained that they always bathed themselves at home and at school and were embarrassed by the insistence of the staff that they bath with an attendant. One positive feature of regional colleges would be that parents would live within relatively easy travelling distance and day sessions could be held for them at the College. An interchange of ideas and experiences could prove extremely useful to the young people concerned.

This chapter has discussed some of the issues that arise in the further education of young people with special needs. Some of the main issues are summarized below.

- Provision for further education on a regional basis for young people with special needs may alleviate some of the shortcomings of the present system of provision and referral to such provision.

- Students who are considered, and themselves feel, able to benefit from ordinary further education should be encouraged to do so. Aids and adaptations and a willingness to accommodate them by members of the staff will be needed. Appropriate specialist support should be available both in ordinary colleges and, where it is not already, in the specialist colleges. Suitable new courses need to be developed.

- An assessment by a team of professionals in close collaboration

with the educational provisions available may be a more effective
and efficient way of assessing the needs and potential of disabled
young people.

- The importance of staff training was considered in the Warnock
  Report (op.cit.) and the inclusion of training for children with
  special needs in initial teacher-training and in-service courses
  should be emphasized. Specialist training for those people concerned with the residential element in specialist colleges is as
  important. Some students, for example, the hearing impaired,
  those with communication disorders and those with personal and
  emotional problems will need comprehensive support. Teachers
  and parents may perceive a need, but feel ill-equipped to deal with
  it.

- An exchange of information and ideas between parents and college
  staff may help to minimize misunderstandings and help to provide
  the young people with support at an important time in their personal development.

- Social education is certainly an area that has been given much
  thought as part of a further education curriculum and disabled
  young people may be particularly likely to benefit from such a
  development.

APPENDIX A

National Foundation for Educational Research in England and Wales

<u>**STRICTLY CONFIDENTIAL**</u>

NAME: _____

Please put a circle around the answer that is right for you.

E.g.   (YES)   NO   when your answer is YES

or

(1)

2   when your answer is next to number 1

3

4

---

1   Are you working at the moment?

YES   NO

If you've answered NO, please move on to question number 5.

2 Are you satisfied with the job you're doing?

> YES   NO

Why is that?

3 Do you expect to be doing the same kind of work in 3 years' time?

> YES   NO   DON'T KNOW

4 What is your employer's name and address?

May I contact your employer and ask him/her to complete a short questionnaire?

> YES   NO

Now please move on to question number 7.

5 Do you have a job fixed up to start in the future?

> YES   NO

If you've answered YES, please move on to question 7.

6 Have you worked at all since you left St Loye's?

> YES   NO

If you've answered NO, please move on to question number 13.

7 Now I want to ask about the *FIRST* job you had after leaving St Loye's. It may be the one you're doing now or one you've left or one you've got fixed up.

What's the job called?

What do you actually do in this job?

What's your take-home pay each week?

Please tick the appropriate box.

☐ £1–£20   ☐ £20–£40   ☐ £40–£60   ☐ £60+

How did you hear about the job?

How long does it take you to get to work?

How many hours a week do you work?

When did you leave (if applicable)?

Why did you leave (if applicable)?

If you've just fixed up your first job since leaving St Loye's please move on to question number 10.

8   Did the job turn out as you thought it would?

YES   NO

If NO, why was this?

If you've only had one job since leaving St Loye's please move on to question number 10.

9   Please complete the table on the next page starting with the *SECOND* job you had since leaving St Loye's. Please give details of *ALL* the jobs you have had.

10   Did you get a job straight away after leaving St Loye's or were you without work for any reason?

Job straight away	1
Without work as was ill	2
Without work as couldn't find a job	3
Other	4

If Other – why was that?

11   If you didn't get a job straight away how long were (or have you been) without work?

Approximately how many weeks/months?

12   Have you ever had any difficulties at work that were because of your disability?

If YES, please give details.

Now move on to question number 18.

13   Why do you think you haven't got a job?

14   Are you interested in finding a job at the moment?
            YES   NO
If NO, why is that?

If YES, what have you done?

	Name of job?	When did you start?	Take-home pay	How did you hear about job?	How many hours per week worked?	How long does it take to travel to work?	When did you leave? (if applicable)	Why did you leave? (if applicable)
Second Job								
Third Job (if applicable)								
Fourth Job (if applicable)								
Fifth Job (if applicable)								
Sixth Job (if applicable)								

15 Have you been able to do anything about finding a job?
        YES   NO
    If NO, why is that?

    If YES, what have you done?

16 What, if anything, do you dislike about not working?

17 What, if anything, do you like about not working?

18 Did you have a job (including part-time work) before you went
    to St Loye's?
        YES   NO
    If YES, what was the job?

    What did you actually do?

    Roughly how many hours a week did you work?

19 Have you had any contact with these people about looking for a
    job? Contact might be by letter, telephone, interview or through
    printed leaflets. Please tick the columns as appropriate.

	No Contact	Contact but of no actual help	Contact useful
Careers Officer/ Youth Employment Officer			
Disablement Resettlement Officer			
Teacher/School			
Family or Friends			
St Loye's			
Someone else			

If you had contact with someone else, please say who it was.

20   Are you satisfied with the help you have had in looking for work?
                YES   NO
      If NO, why is that?

21   How did you first hear about St Loye's?
                Teacher/School   1
                Careers Officer/Youth Employment Officer   2
                Newspaper   3
                Relative or Friend   4
                Other   5
      If Other, please say how.

22   When you were at St Loye's would you say you were
                Happy most of the time   1
                Happy some of the time   2
                Unhappy some of the time   3
                Unhappy most of the time   4
      Why was that?

23   Did what you learnt in the Further Education Unit give you
      any idea of what it's like working and living in the adult world?
                Yes – it was very useful   1
                Yes – it was quite useful   2
                Yes – but I didn't find it much help   3
                No   4

24   If you were running the Further Education Unit what changes
      would you make to help people like you to get jobs or be
      happier?

25   Do you feel, looking back, that it was worth your while to take
      the Further Education course?
                YES   NO
      Why was that?

26   What did you enjoy most about the Further Education course?

27   What did you find most useful about the Further Education
      course?

28   Is there anything you think you'd rather have not done on the
      Further Education course?

29   Is there any special help that you would have liked at St Loye's
      that you didn't have? This could be educational, medical,
      personal or any other sort of help.

                YES   NO

      If YES, could you please say what sort of help?

30   The next questions are concerned with how much difficulty, if
      any, you have in these situations. Having difficulty means that
      you feel ANXIOUS or UNCOMFORTABLE either because
      you don't know what to do or because you feel frightened,
      embarrassed or self-conscious. Some people have said they find
      these situations difficult, others don't – please select the choice
      of difficulty which fits how you feel and write the number of
      your choice in the column.

No difficulty	Slight difficulty	Moderate difficulty	Great difficulty	Avoidance if possible
0	1	2	3	4

(1)   Mixing with people at work/college.
(2)   Making friends of your own age.
(3)   Going out with someone you are attracted to.
(4)   Being with a group containing both men and women of
      roughly the same age as you.
(5)   Entertaining people in your home, lodgings, etc.
(6)   Going into a room full of people.
(7)   Meeting strangers.
(8)   Approaching others – making the first move and starting
      up a friendship.
(9)   Making ordinary decisions affecting others (e.g. what to
      do together in the evening).
(10) Taking the initiative and keeping a conversation going.
(11) Looking at people directly in the eyes.
(12) People looking at you.
(13) Talking about yourself and your feelings in a
      conversation.

31   Have there been any changes in your health since you were at
     St Loye's?

YES – health is worse	1
YES – health had improved	2
NO	3

     If YES, could you please give some details.

32   Are you registered with the Department of Employment as a
     disabled person?

     YES   NO   DON'T KNOW

     Thank you very much.

APPENDIX B

National Foundation for Educational Research in England and Wales

STRICTLY CONFIDENTIAL

Name of employee: _____

Name of firm/organisation: _____

Position held: _____

Please circle the correct answer where necessary.

1   How many employees are there in your organisation? _____

2   Have you known or employed other people with the same disability as this employee?
          YES   NO
If YES, please give details.

3   Was a Careers Officer or Disablement Resettlement Officer involved in the placing of this employee?
          YES   NO
If YES   Do you feel that the Disablement Resettlement Officer or Careers Officer gave a realistic assessment of this employee's suitability for the job?
          YES   NO
If NO, please give details.

4   Why did you decide to employ this particular employee?

5   Would you say that this employee's work has been
      better than you expected   1
      not as good as you expected   2
      about the same as you expected   3

6   Would you say that this employee had been adequately
     prepared for work when he/she started?
              YES   NO

7   Do you have or have you had employees with other kinds of
     disability than this employee?
              YES   NO
     If YES, please give details.

8   Have any adaptations been made at work either for this
     employee or other disabled people?
              YES   NO
     If YES, please give details.

9   Has the employee had any accidents at work?
              YES   NO
     If YES, please give details.

10   Has this employee had more time off, with illness, compared
     with other employees?
              YES   NO

11   Does this employee's disability affect his/her work at all?
              YES   NO
     If YES, please give details.

12   Would you say you get a fair day's work from this employee as
     compared to able-bodied employees?
              YES   NO
     If NO, please give details.

13   Would you, in view of your experience, consider employing a
similarly disabled person in the future?
          YES   NO

As I said before I have tried to keep this brief and I would
welcome any comments from you either with regard to any
problems you may have had with this employee or to any other
points you might like to make.

Thank you very much.

APPENDIX C

Chapter Summaries

Chapter 2

- Less than half of the young people were currently in open employment although two-thirds of them had obtained such work since leaving St Loye's.

- Of those people who obtained open employment 62 per cent had only had one job and 26 per cent had had two jobs. Seventy-two per cent had been in employment for over 50 per cent of the time, indeed 36 per cent had been employed for over 90 per cent of the time.

- A first placement was not necessarily a crucial determinant of future placements in that some young people with short initial placements went on to have stable work histories and a stable first placement did not always result in a stable placement in employment over all.

- For a third of the young people the wages earned suggested that there were incentives other than financial that led them to obtain work.

- Some interesting trends emerged from a comparison of the young people who had obtained open employment in that those young people whose handicap affected their presentation to other people and their mobility were less likely to have obtained open employment or to be currently so employed.

- There were a substantial number of people who, having obtained open employment or indeed skill-related open employment, had subsequently left it. The reasons for leaving are detailed at the end of the section on open employment. Clearly the main reason why people left employment – redundancy or job closure – reflects wider political and economic issues. The number of young people who wrote that they had been sacked was extremely small and corresponds with the comments of employers discussed earlier in this chapter. A substantial minority (45 per cent) left work for reasons that related to their disability or because they were dissatisfied with the work. More efficient job placings may counter at least some of this trend.

- The Youth Opportunities Programme had not proved to be a way into permanent employment for the small number of young people who had been involved. In the light of rising levels of youth unemployment the direction of the YOP may need rethinking.

- The employment of the few young men in sheltered work was discussed and the need for appropriate placing was stressed.

- There were five young people attending adult training centres although this provision is generally considered to be suitable for mentally handicapped people. There would seem to be a need for more appropriate provision for young physically handicapped people with hostel accommodation if required.

- Over all 70 per cent of the young people who took a training course had obtained open employment. Those with a commercial training were more likely to obtain work that was related to their training trade.

- Of those young people who had not taken a training course 56 per cent had obtained open employment and 72 per cent of these had been employed for more than 80 per cent of the time.

- Of the young people who had not completed the course, a majority (67 per cent) had obtained open employment. Offering these young people a modified course may be beneficial.

- A large minority of young people (45 per cent) did not however obtain open employment that was related to their training trade. At the time of this study, 51 per cent of young people in open employment were in jobs related to their training trade. There may well be merit in extending the training curriculum to include the job-related skills proposed by some of the respondents and discussed in Chapter Six. The FEU curriculum development discussed in Chapter Three may provide realistic alternatives. Clearly the relevance of a specific training lessens the longer a person is unemployed. The young people interviewed in this study who were unemployed were in the main looking for any work even though they may have wanted to work in their training trade when they left St Loye's.

- The difficulties that young people reported at work were in many cases surmountable by changes in the job content or environment or by providing support at the appropriate time.

- The comments made by the present employers of the young people were overwhelmingly positive. Eighty-one per cent felt that they got a fair day's work from their employee and 85 per cent that they would, in view of their experience, consider employing a similar disabled person in the future.

- The young people had good work records in terms of accidents at work and extra time off with illness. Of those employees whose disability was said to affect their work, the restriction was minimal in most cases.

- Only eight employers felt that their employee's work had not been as good as they expected and of the others, over half felt that it was better. Employers wrote of the personal qualities and attainments that had made them decide to engage their employee and a few specifically made reference to the employment of disabled people.

Chapter 3

- The vast majority of young people currently in employment felt that they were satisfied with their work and the most frequently given reason why related to the content of the work. The caution was added that this satisfaction may be relatively short-lived, particularly for those young people with limited opportunities for promotion. Half of the respondents did not know whether or not they would be doing the same kind of work in three years' time.

- There was considerable 'fit' between the work aspirations of the young people interviewed and their present or hoped-for employment. The importance of the satisfaction they had gained from the education and training at St Loye's was mentioned.

- The unemployed young people provided evidence of the boredom, financial difficulty and feeling of uselessness that unemployment can bring.

- The dilemma of finding a balance between discouraging young people in terms of employment and presenting them with an unrealistic goal was discussed. It was suggested that a broadened revised curriculum may be advantageous.

Chapter 4

- Information collected about how people heard about jobs they had obtained showed the use made of the Jobcentre and family and friends.

- The usefulness of the professional placing services even when they did not provide information about jobs obtained was indicated by the young people in this study.

- A third of the young people, many of whom are in employment, expressed some dissatisfaction with the help available to them. Several comments related to lack of encouragement or time given by staff in the placement services.

- The importance of public education about disabled people was discussed and it was said that the professional placement services have an important role to play.

- The considerable efforts made by those young people currently unemployed to obtain work were discussed.

Chapter 5

- The concept of stigma and the tendency to group all disabled people together with an emphasis on their disability rather than their individuality was discussed. The confusion and ill-informed opinions that many able-bodied people express create particular problems for disabled people.

- The desire expressed by young people in this study to be treated as 'normal' human beings was commented on and the skills that they could usefully learn in order to manage their interactions with able-bodied people were mentioned. Able-bodied people may respond inappropriately in unfamiliar encounters with disabled people and a disabled person has to be able to deal with this and sometimes with unpleasantness.

- The social isolation of many of the young people was commented upon and it was suggested that many of them were able to mix socially when given suitable opportunities.

- Most people did not structure their time – membership of clubs and organizations was limited as was attendance at evening classes – and many were dissatisfied with their social life.

- Most of the interviewees were living with their parents and many expressed dissatisfaction with doing so, either because of their immediate or long-term concerns. The need for young people to gain a degree of independence was discussed.

- The need for emotional independence was stressed and the personal problems of some of the young people in this study were mentioned. Comment was made on the role that counselling could play.

- The scores of the young people who rated their own social interaction skills suggest that there are areas of interaction that could usefully be included in a programme of social skills training.

- Training may be of considerable benefit to the 12 per cent of young people who rated themselves as having quite severe social handicap and could ease the social and vocational development of many of the others.

Chapter 6

- The majority of young people felt that they had been happy most of the time whilst in the Further Education Unit. The most frequently given reason for this was the opportunity to make friends and to have an enjoyable social life. A specialist college may provide young people with the chance to gain from peer group support at this important stage in their development.

- When asked what changes they would make to the Further Education Unit, 33 per cent of the young people suggested changes that would prepare them for employment. Visits to work places, work experience, mock interviews, careers guidance and placing help were all mentioned.

- Eighty-eight per cent of the young people who had had open employment felt that it had been worth their while to take the Further Education course, as did 82 per cent of those who had not been so employed. Perceptions of the usefulness of the course were not coloured either by employment history or current employment status.

- The most frequently given reason why the course had been worthwhile was that it had provided a valuable opportunity to learn. The benefits obtained from small classes and individual attention were mentioned by several people.

- Of the 14 per cent of young people who did not feel that the course had been worthwhile most felt that they had not learnt much from it or that their time could have been better spent looking for employment.

- Literacy and numeracy skills were specifically mentioned by 27 per cent of the young people as being the most useful aspect of the course. Indeed 16 per cent had found them the most enjoyable part. Gains in these basic skills may have been implicit in many of the comments about opportunities to learn.

Chapter 7

- Provision for further education on a regional basis for young people with special needs may alleviate some of the shortcomings of the present system of provision and referral to such provision.

- Students who are considered, and themselves feel, able to benefit from ordinary further education should be encouraged to do so. Aids and adaptations and a willingness to accommodate them by members of the staff will be needed. Appropriate specialist support should be available both in ordinary colleges and, where it is not already, in the specialist colleges. Suitable new courses need to be developed.

- An assessment by a team of professionals in close collaboration with the educational provisions available may be a more effective and efficient way of assessing the needs and potential of disabled young people.

- The importance of staff training was considered in the Warnock Report (op.cit.) and the inclusion of training for children with special needs in initial teacher training and in-service courses should be emphasized. Specialist training for those people concerned with the residential element in specialist colleges is as important. Some students, for example the hearing impaired, those with communication disorders and those with personal and emotional problems will need comprehensive support. Teachers and parents may perceive a need, but feel ill-equipped to deal with it.

- An exchange of information and ideas between parents and college staff may help to minimize misunderstandings and help to provide the young people with support at an important time in their personal development.

- Social education is certainly an area that has been given much thought as part of a further education curriculum and disabled young people may be particularly likely to benefit from such a development.

References and Bibliography

AGERHOLM, M. (1975). 'A Nomenclature and Classification of Intrinsic Handicaps', *Royal Society of Health Journal*, 1975, **95**, 1, 3–8.

ARGYLE, M. (1967). *The Psychology of Interpersonal Behaviour*. London: Allen Lane: The Penguin Press.

ASSOCIATION FOR SPINA BIFIDA AND HYDROCEPHA- LUS. (1978). *Children with Spina Bifida at School*. London: ASBAH.

BARNES, J. A. (1978). *Preparing for Employment: A Model Pro- gramme for the Handicapped School Leaver*. Salford: City of Salford Education Department.

BLEACKLEY, R. (Ed) (1974). *Despite Disability: Career Achieve- ment by Handicapped People*. Reading: Educational Explorers.

BLECK, E. E. and NAGEL, D. A. (1975). *Physically Handicapped Children: A Medical Atlas for Teachers*. New York: Grüne and Stratton.

BOSWELL, M. and WINGROVE, J. (Eds) (1974). *The Handi- capped Person in the Community*. Tavistock Publications in associa- tion with The Open University Press.

BRANNEN, P. (Ed) (1975). *Entering the world of work: some sociological perspectives*. London: HMSO.

BRITISH EPILEPSY ASSOCIATION. *Epilepsy '79. Epilepsy '78.* Wokingham: British Epilepsy Association.

BROOKS, N. A. (1980). 'The Social Consequences of Disability', *Teaching Sociology*, **7**, 4, July 1980, 425–38.

BROWNE, G. (undated). Assessment for Work Readiness: A Booklet for use with Slow Learners Attending Work Orientated Courses at Colleges of Further Education and at Industrial Training Workshops. Bridgend: Bridgend College of Technology. (mimeographed).

BROWNE, G. (1977). *Adjustment to Industry for Less-Able School Leavers: The Bridgend Project*. Manchester: National Elfrida Rathbone Society.

BROWNE, G. (1978a). The development of a procedure for assessing the readiness of ESN school leavers for open employment. Unpublished B.Ed. Dissertation, University of Wales.

BROWNE, G. (1978b). *Continuing Education: A Programme for the Less-Able in Colleges of Further Education*. Manchester: National Elfrida Rathbone Society.

BROWNE, G. (1978c). 'What type of further education?' *Special Education: Forward Trends*, **5**, 4, 8–9.

BROWNE, G. (1979). Some Considerations Relating to Post School Education for Intellectually Impaired Adolescents at Colleges of Further Education. Paper presented at International Cerebral Palsy Conference: Leaving School in the 1980s. University College, Oxford.

BULLETIN OF THE EUROPEAN COMMUNITIES. (1976). Supplement 12/76. *From Education to Working Life*. Luxembourg: European Communities Commission.

CANTOR, L. M. and ROBERTS, I. F. (1979). *Further Education Today: A Critical Review*. London: Routledge and Kegan Paul.

CARTER, M. P. (1962). *Home, School and Work*. Oxford: Pergamon.

CARVER, V. and RODDA, M. (1978) *Disability and the Environment*. London: Paul Elek.

CCETSW (CENTRAL COUNCIL FOR EDUCATION AND TRAINING IN SOCIAL WORK). (1974). *Social Work: People with Handicaps Need Better Trained Workers*. CCETSW Paper 5.

CHERRY, N. (1974). 'Do Careers Officers give good advice?' *British Journal of Guidance and Counselling*. January 1974, **2**, 1, 27–40.

CLARKE, L. (1977). *The Practice of Vocational Guidance: A Review of UK Research Literature*. July 1977, Report No. 35. MSC Employment Service Agency.

CLARKE, L. (1978). *The Transition from School to Work: A Critical Review of UK Research Literature*. Report No. 49. Feb. 1978. MSC.

COE, D. (1978). *Opportunities for Handicapped Students in Post-School Education*. London: The Association of Colleges for Further and Higher Education. (pamphlet).

COE, D. (1979). Planning Further Education Courses for Handicapped Students at National, Regional and Local Level. In: DIXON, K. and HUTCHINSON, D. (Eds). *Further Education for Handicapped Students*. Bolton: Bolton College of Education (Technical).

COOKE, G. (1979). The Implications of Warnock for Further Education. In: DIXON, K. and HUTCHINSON, D. (Ibid.).

COMMITTEE APPOINTED BY THE SECRETARY OF STATE FOR SCOTLAND. (1975). *The Secondary Education of Physically Handicapped Children in Scotland*. London: HMSO. (McCann Report).

COMMITTEE OF ENQUIRY INTO THE EDUCATION OF HANDICAPPED CHILDREN AND YOUNG PEOPLE. (1978). *Special Educational Needs*. (Warnock Report). London: HMSO.

DAVOUD, N. and KETTLE, M. (1980). *Multiple Sclerosis and its effect upon employment*. London: Multiple Sclerosis Society.

DEPARTMENT OF EDUCATION AND SCIENCE. (1979). *A Better Start in Working Life – Vocational Preparation for employed young people in Great Britain*. London: DES.

DES Circular 6/76. Welsh Office Circular 10 4/76, Government Statement on Unified Vocational Preparation (21 July 1976) and Scottish Education Department Circular 959 (21 July 1976).

DES Circular 10/77. Welsh Office Circular 165/77. Unemployed Young People: The Contribution of the Education Service (30 September 1977) and Scottish Education Department Circular 996 (7 October 1977).

DEPARTMENT OF EMPLOYMENT. (1971). *Services for the Disabled*. London: HMSO.

DISABILITY ALLIANCE. (1978). *Disability Rights Handbook for 1978*. From The Disability Alliance, 5, Netherhall Gardens, London NW3.

DIXON, K. and HUTCHINSON, D. (Eds). (1979). *Further Education for Handicapped Students*. Bolton: Bolton College of Education (Technical).

DORNER, S. (1976). 'Adolescents with Spina Bifida – How they see their situation', *Archives of Disease in Childhood*, 51, 439.

DORNER, S. (1977). 'Problems of Teenagers', *Physiotherapy*, June 1977, 63, No. 6.

DORNER, S. (1975). 'The relationship of physical handicap to stress in families with an adolescent with spina bifida', *Develop. Med. Child. Neurol.*, 17, 765–76.

DUBROW, A. (1965). 'Attitudes towards disability', *Journal of Rehabilitation*, **31**, July/August, 25–6.

DYER, Philip. (1979). 'One Potato, Two Potato, Three Potato, Four – Leaving School in the 1980's', *Talk given to the International Cerebral Palsy Society*, University College, Oxford, 25–8, March 1979.

DUCK, S. (1980). 'With a little help from my friends', *New Society*, 30 October.

ELLIMAN, D. (1978). 'Epilepsy and the school leavers' medical', *The Lancet*, reproduced in *Epilepsy*, '78, 35–7. Wokingham: British Epilepsy Association.

FALLON, B. (1979). *Able to Work*, London: Spinal Injuries Association.

FEU (FURTHER EDUCATION CURRICULUM REVIEW AND DEVELOPMENT UNIT). (1979). *A Basis for Choice*. London: FEU.

FEU (FURTHER EDUCATION CURRICULUM REVIEW AND DEVELOPMENT UNIT). (1980). *Beyond Coping: some approaches to social education*. London: FEU.

FRASER, B. C. (1977). 'Integration'. *Child: Care, health and development*, **3**, 3, 201–11.

FRASER, J. M. (1971). *Psychology. General – Industrial – Social*. London: Sir Isaac Pitman.

GERBER, P. and GRIFFITHS, H. (1980). Letter to *Developmental Medicine and Child Neurology*, 22, 686–7.

GLANVILLE, R. A. (1974). The Education, Training and Employment of the Handicapped School-leaver. Unpublished M.Ed. Thesis, University of Reading.

GOFFMAN, E. (1963). *Stigma: Notes on the Management of a Spoiled Identity*. Englewood Cliffs, New Jersey: Prentice-Hall Inc., 1–40.

GREAVES, Mary. (1972). 'The Employment of Disabled People', *Community Health*, **3**, 4, 175–80.

GREAVES, M. and MASSIE, B. (1977). *Work and Disability 1977*. London: The Disabled Living Foundation.

HARRIS, A., COX, E. and SMITH, R. W. (1971). *Handicapped and Impaired in Great Britain*, Part I. London: HMSO.

HILBOURNE, J.(1972). 'On Disabling the Normal – The Implication of Physical Disability for Other People', *Br. J. Social Work*, **2**, 4, 497–504.

HILL, M. J. *et al*. (1973). *'Men Out of Work' A Study of Unemploy-*

ment in 3 English Towns. Cambridge University Press.

HOLLAND REPORT. (1977). See under: MANPOWER SERVICES COMMISSION.

HUNT, G. (1981). 'Spina Bifida: Implications for 100 Children at School', *Developmental Medicine and Child Neurology.*, 23, 160–72.

HUTCHINSON, D. and CLEGG, N. (1972). 'Experiment in Further Education', *Special Education*, 61, No. 3.

HUTCHINSON, D. and CLEGG, N. (1975). 'Orientated towards Work', *Special Education*, 2, No. 1, 22–5.

INDUSTRIAL TRAINING RESEARCH UNIT LTD (ITRU). (1979). *The A–Z Study Differences between improvers and non-improvers among young unskilled workers*. ITRU Publication SY4.

INTO WORK. (1981). *Jobless – a study of unemployment in North Tyneside*. Into Work Research Project.

KARLSSON, B., GARDENSTROM, L., NORDQUIST, I. and JACOBSON, F. (1965). 'Cerebral Palsy in Young Adults', *Develop. Med. Child. Neurol.*, 7, 269–77.

KEIL, E. T. (1976). *The Induction of School Leavers into Work in Leicestershire*. Leicestershire Committee for Education and Industry.

KELLAWAY, G. P. (1967). *'Education for living'*. Cambridge University Press.

KETTLE, M. (1979a). *Management Policies Relative to the Employment of Disabled People*. unpublished report. University of Bradford.

KETTLE, M. (1979b). *Disabled People and their Employment. A Review of Research into the Performance of Disabled People at Work*. Association of Disabled Professionals.

MAIZELS, J. (1970). *Adolescent Needs and the Transition from School to Work*. London: Athlone Press.

MANPOWER SERVICES COMMISSION. (1977). *Young People and Work*. Report on the feasibility of a new programme of opportunities for unemployed young people. (The Holland Report). London: Manpower Services Commission.

MANPOWER SERVICES COMMISSION AND NATIONAL ADVISORY COUNCIL ON EMPLOYMENT OF DISABLED PEOPLE. (1977). *Positive Policies*. London: Manpower Services Commission or HMSO.

MANPOWER SERVICES COMMISSION. (1980). *Instructional Guide to Social and Life Skills*. London: MSC.

MARSHALL, T. and OLIVER, M. (1979). *Work and Disability: An Employment Survey of Paraplegics and Tetraplegics*. London: Spinal Injuries Association.

MORRIS, P. (1974). Learning together in Worksop, *Community Care*, 13, 14–15.

MITTLER, P. (Ed). (1970). *The Psychological Assessment of Mental and Physical Handicaps*. London: Methuen and Co. Ltd.

NATIONAL ASSOCIATION OF TEACHERS IN FURTHER AND HIGHER EDUCATION. (1978). College Provision for Handicapped Students: Report of a Survey, 1685–78. London: NATFHE. (mimeographed).

NATIONAL ASSOCIATION OF TEACHERS IN FURTHER AND HIGHER EDUCATION. (1978). 'NATFHE sceptical about DES commitment', *Education*, 22, 600.

NATIONAL ASSOCIATION OF TEACHERS IN FURTHER AND HIGHER EDUCATION. (1979). Special Educational Needs: A Response to The Warnock Report. London: NATFHE. (mimeographed).

NATIONAL BUREAU FOR HANDICAPPED STUDENTS (NBHS). (1977, 1978). *An Educational Policy for Handicapped People*. London: NBHS. From the NBHS, c/o Middlesex Polytechnic, All Saints Site, White Hart Lane, London N17.

NATIONAL BUREAU FOR HANDICAPPED STUDENTS. (1979). Response to The Warnock Report on Special Education. London: NBHS. (mimeographed)

NATIONAL INNOVATIONS CENTRE. (1974). Disabled Students in Higher Education, N.I.C. (Out of print. Copies available in some libraries.)

NATIONAL UNION OF STUDENTS AND ACTION RESEARCH FOR THE CRIPPLED CHILD. (1976). *The Disabled Student*. London: NUS AND ARCC.

O'MOORE, M. (1980). 'Social Acceptance of the physically handicapped child in the ordinary school', *Child: Care, health and development*, 6, 317–37.

ORGANISATION FOR ECONOMIC CO-OPERATION AND DEVELOPMENT. (1978). *The Education of the Handicapped Adolescent*, An Interim Report of the First Phase of the Project. Paris: OECD.

ORTON, C. (1979). *The Child with a Medical Problem in the Ordinary School*. London: Home and School Council.

OSWIN, M. (1978). *Holes in the Welfare Net.* Bedford Square Press of the National Council of Social Science.

PANCKHURST, J. and McALLISTER, A. (1980). *An Approach to the Further Education of the Physically Handicapped.* Slough: National Foundation For Educational Research.

PANCKHURST, J. (1980). *Focus on Physical Handicap. Provision for young people with special needs in further education.* Slough: National Foundation For Educational Research.

THE QUEEN ELIZABETH'S FOUNDATION FOR THE DIS-ABLED. (1972). *Handicapped School Leavers.* Leatherhead, Surrey: The Queen Elizabeth's Foundation for the Disabled.

REGIONAL ADVISORY COUNCIL FOR THE ORGANISA-TION OF FURTHER EDUCATION IN THE EAST MID-LANDS. (1981). *Opportunities for Further Education for those with Special Educational Needs.* Nottingham: East Midlands RAC.

REGIONAL ADVISORY COUNCIL FOR THE ORGANISA-TION OF FURTHER EDUCATION IN THE EAST MID-LANDS. (1981). *Further Education for Handicapped People 1980.* Nottingham: East Midlands RAC.

REYNOLDS, D. (1980). 'Employing the young disabled', *Community Care*, 21 August, 20–2.

ROBERTS, K. (1977). 'The social conditions, consequences, and limitations of careers guidance', *British Journal of Guidance and Counselling*, **5**, 1, January 1977.

RODDA, M. (1970). *The Hearing Impaired School Leaver.* University of London Press.

ROE, A. (1956). *The Psychology of Occupations.* New York: J Wiley & Sons.

ROWAN, P. (1980). *What Sort of Life?* A paper for the OECD project 'The Handicapped Adolescent'. Slough: National Foundation for Educational Research.

ROWE, B. and MORGAN, B. (1976). 'Care for the Handicapped Adult', *Social Work Today*, **7**, No. 5, 134–6.

RUTTER, M. (1980). 'Growing up in a changing world', *New Society*, 17 April, 98–9.

SCHARFF, D. E. and HILL, J. M. M. (1976). *Between 2 Worlds, Aspects of the transition from school to work.* London: Careers Consultants Ltd.

SNOWDON WORKING PARTY REPORT. (1976). *Integrating the Disabled.* THORPE-TRACE, R. (Ed). Horsham: National Fund for Research into Crippling Diseases.

SPEAKE, B. and WHELAN, E. (1977). Work Preparation Courses are helping handicapped school leavers find permanent jobs. *Department of Employment Gazette*, 803–5.

SPEAKE, B. and WHELAN, E. (1979). *Young Persons Work Preparation Course – A systematic evaluation*. Manpower Services Commission Employment Service Agency.

STOWELL, R. (1980). *Disabled People on Supplementary Benefit*. London: Social Science Research Council.

STUBBINS, J. (Ed). (1977). *Social and Psychological Aspects of Disability. A Handbook for Practitioners*. University Park Press.

THOMAS, E. (1964). *The Handicapped School Leaver*. London: British Council for Rehabilitation of the Disabled.

TOPLISS, E. (1975). *Provision for the Disabled*. Oxford: Blackwell.

TROWBRIDGE TECHNICAL COLLEGE. (1980). *Assessment and Work Preparation Course*. Trowbridge: Trowbridge Technical College.

TROWER, P., BRYANT, B. and ARGYLE, M. (1978). *Social Skills and Mental Health*. London: Methuen.

TURNER, J. (1980). 'A Springboard to Work', *New Society*, 30 October, 230–1.

TUCKEY, L., PARFIT, J., TUCKEY, B. (1973). *Handicapped School Leavers – Their Further Education, Training and Employment*. Slough: National Foundation for Educational Research.

WALKER, A. and SINFIELD, A. (1975). 'Unemployment and the Disabled', *Poverty*, No. 32, 15–19.

WALKER, A. (1976). 'The Hardest Job', *Community Care*, 1 December, 20–2.

WALKER, A. and LEWIS, P. (1977). 'Careers Advice and Employment Experience of a Small Group of Handicapped School Leavers', *Careers Quarterly*, **29**, 1, 5–14.

WALKER, A. (1980). 'The Handicapped School Leaver and the transition to work', *Br. J. of Guidance and Counselling*, **8**, 2, July.

WARNOCK REPORT. (1978). See under: COMMITTEE OF ENQUIRY INTO THE EDUCATION OF HANDICAPPED CHILDREN AND YOUNG PEOPLE.

WEIR, S. (1981). 'Our image of the disabled, how ready we are to help', *New Society*, 1 January, 7–10.

WEST, P. (1981). 'From bad to worse: people's experience and stereotypes of epilepsy', *Epilepsy '81*. Wokingham: British Epilepsy Association.

WOODBURN, M. (1975). *Social Implications of Spina Bifida*. Slough: National Foundation for Educational Research.

YOUNGHUSBAND, E., DAVIE, R., BIRCHALL, D. and KELL-MER PRINGLE, M. (1970). *Living with Handicap*. National Bureau for Co-operation in Child Care.

YOUTH, A.I.D. (1980). *Annual Report 1979–80*. London: Youth A.I.D.

Index